THE ULTIMATE WEDDING

Christ & His Bride

Catherine Jinadu

Copyright © 2023 by Catherine Jinadu

Independently Published
ISBN 9798389103214

New Covenant Church
Nigeria National Administrative Office
P.M.B. 5450, Dugbe
Ibadan, Nigeria
www.newcovenantchurchnigeria.org

New Covenant Church Logistics
9606 East Foothill Blvd.
Rancho Cucamonga, CA 91730
(909) 791-8095 www.nccworld.org

Unless otherwise stated, all Scripture quotations are taken from the New King James Version®. Copyright © 1982 by Thomas Nelson. Used by permission.

Scripture quotations marked NIV are from the Holy Bible, New International Version®, NIV®. Copyright © 1973, 1978, 1984, 2011 by Biblica, Inc.™ Used by permission of Zondervan.

Scripture quotations marked TPT are from The Passion Translation®. Copyright © 2017, 2018, 2020 by Passion & Fire Ministries, Inc. Used by permission. All rights reserved.

To Zoë, Isabelle and Amy

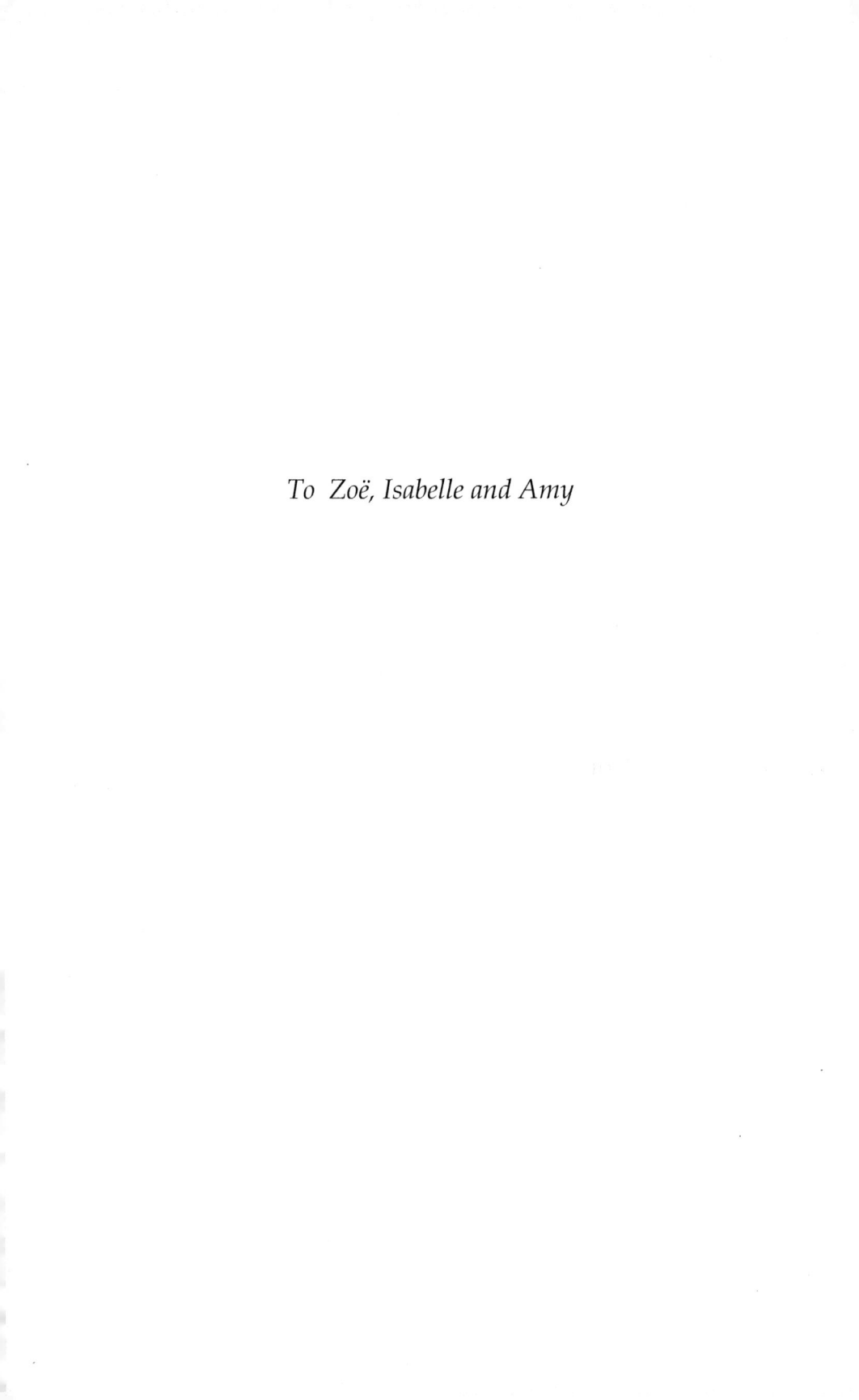

Acknowledgements

I am grateful to God for my husband of 57 years, Paul, for exemplifying the manliness, vigour, and protection of an earthly bridegroom!

I thank God for our two sons Philip and Simon, and God's promise to me, "Instead of your fathers will be your sons whom you shall make princes in all the earth." (Psalm 45:16) And for their wives Kate and Helen and their children.

I say a big "Thank you" to our friend Bruce Oliver for his booklet, *The Power of the Blood of Jesus* which greatly informed the writing of the chapter *The Seven Wounds of Jesus*.

Contents

PART ONE: INTRODUCING...   9
    1. Jesus Christ, Special Agent   11

PART TWO: TYPES AND SHADOWS   19
    2. Rebekah, the Willing Bride   21
    3. Ruth, the Servant Bride   26
    4. David, the Worshiping Bride   37
    5. David, the Warrior Bride   46
    6. Bathsheba, the Forgiving Bride   55
    7. Esther, the Valiant Bride   65

PART THREE: THE BRIDE PRICE   72
    8. The Cost to the Father   73
    9. The Cost to the Son   77
    10. The Seven Wounds of Jesus   82

PART FOUR: OUR HEAVENLY BRIDEGROOM   91
    11. Beholding Our King   93
    12. The Glories of the Messiah and His Bride   101
    13. The Bride's Dress   106
    14. The Wedding Feast   116
    15. Our Eternal Home   121

    Epilogue   127
    Endnotes   131
    About the Author   133

PART ONE
Introducing...

1
Jesus Christ, Special Agent

The Bible is such a treasure trove, and those who love it are invited to a treasure hunt. As we search the Scriptures, we find priceless nuggets of pure gold. What Winston Churchill said of Russia is also true of the Bible: *"It is a riddle wrapped in a mystery inside an enigma!"*[1] Let's hunt together from Genesis to Revelation, discovering the greatest love story ever told; a love that will continue to be revealed throughout all eternity.

It's not only a love story, but also a thriller, an exciting and captivating narrative. It's the story of a Secret Agent sent from a faraway Kingdom to rescue His bride. And who is that bride? Dear reader, it's YOU! Rescued from whom? Rescued from what? Put simply, from the Evil Enemy and his Evil Empire. The Bible narrative is all about the Lord Jesus Christ, from beginning to end:

> "In the volume of the book it is written of Me,"[2] He declares.

But surprisingly, this story is also our story. It begins in Genesis and ends in Revelation.

Before Time

Scene One begins in timeless space. Here we find the Kingdom of Heaven, a kingdom pulsating with beauty, inhabited by a hundred million angelic beings where cherubim and seraphim glow with blazing fire. Here the King is God the Father. Yes, there is a family in heaven,[3] but there is only one Son. The Son is the express image of the Father's glory[4] and His daily delight. The third member of the family is the Holy Spirit. His heart, like that of the Father, is explosive with love. The Father yearns for many more children, and like any good father, He desires a special bride for His Son.

A family meeting is held, and proposals are put forth. "Let Us, Elohim, create a perfect universe with galaxies, stars by the billions, with trillions of planets and a tiny spec in the Milky Way called Planet Earth. A raging ball of fire will be its sun, its light and warmth. On this small planet, We will create a garden of breathtaking beauty. We will prepare it with trees, grasses, herbs, birds, animals, and fishes. And last of all, We will create mankind in Our Own Image to be just like Us; to rule and reign, to have dominion, to be fruitful to and multiply."

The "six days" of creation may have lasted millions of years, though in God's timing they were indeed six days. No doubt it started with a very BIG BANG! But this bang was orchestrated by God the Father. These were times of vibrant energy, fun and fireworks, as the Holy Trio flung pulsars, quasars, and galaxies into space. This creative burst goes on today as more and more heavenly bodies emerge. We are told that there are five thousand species of mammals and ten thousand species of birds. Reptiles and amphibian species number in the fifteen thousand, fish twenty-six thousand, sixty thousand crustaceans, and a staggering one million insects! But last of all came the creation of man, made in the very image of God.

The Son worked together with the Father as a master Craftsman, daily delighting in His Father and all their creative energy while the Holy Spirit breathed life into their handiwork. It was a time of great rejoicing. We read of when *"the morning stars sang together and all the sons of God [the angels] shouted for joy."* (Job 38:7)

Jesus has this to say:

"When He marked out the foundations of the earth, then I was beside Him as a master craftsman: I was daily His delight, rejoicing always before Him, rejoicing in the inhabited world, and my delight was with the sons of men." (Proverbs 8:30, 31)

As the Apostle John reminds us, the creation came forth as God the Father spoke, Jesus was the Word and the Holy Spirit was the *ruach*, the very breath of God. Each star was named and counted; as many as the grains of sand on every seashore. How long did that take? Only our Father knows but consider this: in the known universe there are two hundred million galaxies. Each consists of anything from one hundred thousand to a trillion stars.

"He counts the number of the stars and calls them all by name." (Psalm 147:4)

Yes, this is indeed the time when you and I were also created. We were, in fact, chosen *"IN CHRIST before the foundation of the world,"*[5] kept back and reserved for the day of our birth. There is a huge library in heaven with a book for every one of us. Each book contains a unique account of our life as God the Father has planned it; the day of our birth, our sex, our features, and personality. God's plan for you is unique to you. Your DNA, iris, and fingerprints are yours alone. The love of Father, Son, and Holy Spirit is so comprehensive, so detailed that it sets our hearts on fire.

Of the ten billion people envisaged each was to be unique and subtlety different: each person a work of art, a poem (Ephesians 2:10). Every person is created in the image and likeness of God, whether male or female. (For indeed, the Triune God has both male and female characteristics.) No two people are the same, each one having their own definitive personality; each one reflecting a differing aspect of the glory of God; each one designed to bring Him unique pleasure.

> "You formed my inward parts; You covered me in my mother's womb. I will praise You, for I am fearfully and wonderfully made. When I was made in secret... Your eyes saw my substance, being yet unformed, and in Your book they all were written, the days fashioned for me, when as yet there were none of them. How precious also are Your thoughts to me, O God! How great is the sum of them! If I should count them, they would be more in number than the (grains of) sand." (Psalm 139:13-18)

As we have seen, each one of us is *"chosen to be **in Christ** before the beginning of the world"* (Ephesians 1:4) Here we have the genesis of the Bride of Christ. (Everyone has been chosen but who will say, "Yes" to Him?) Will you?

So, Adam was made in God's image, glowing with the Shekinah Glory of his Father, and everything around him in the garden was lovely! Except...

It soon became apparent that Adam was occasionally lonely. The problem was that there was no one commensurate with him, no other created being was quite like him.

The First Anaesthetic
Leading to the First Marriage

The Lord God caused a deep sleep to fall on Adam "Ish" and He took from Adam's side a rib. This He fashioned into "Ishah" — a woman! Here were two fully formed adults, but with all the joyful naivety of children happily ruling and reigning in the garden, daily exulting together with the Divine Trinity and the angelic host. Note that Eve was "in" Adam and taken "out of" Adam. She was *"bone of his bone and flesh of his flesh."* (Genesis 2:3)

So, we have a perfect garden, populated with perfect people, enjoying daily fellowship with a perfect God. They are commissioned to rule, to reign, to subdue, to be fruitful and to multiply.[6] Everything around them is for their delight. There is only one prohibition: they should not eat from the tree of the knowledge of good and evil.

Paradise Lost

Enter the Evil Enemy. He entered slimily, seductively, and spectacularly. He looked splendid, like one of the angels, as indeed, he formerly was.[7] Eve was dazzled, caught unawares. Sin soon entered, not only the garden, but into the very heart of the Man and the Woman. In that dreadful hour, everything changed. The Man and the Woman were taken captive. A perfect planet was irrevocably marred. Sin set in and in its train, came death, decay, and destruction. The dominion given to Adam was ceded to Satan, and the government of Planet Earth was transferred to the Evil Enemy and his Evil Empire. It was a disaster of astronomic proportions. The angels wept.

Scene one is narrated in detail for us in Genesis, but let's fast forward to the end of the book—The Revelation of the Lord Jesus Christ. Here we find a new heaven and a new earth. The Evil Enemy and his Evil Empire have been comprehensively defeated. The new earth pulsates with purity and holiness. The relationship between God and man is fully restored. Yes, Father God has the children His heart longed for but wonderfully, these children now become the beautiful bride for His Son. This is a union of spiritual intimacy that will grow in grace and glory forever.

The Second Adam has systematically defeated the machinations of the Evil Enemy. How did it happen? We find the answer in the intervening sixty-four books of the Bible, describing a glorious restoration where the heroic Son of God comes as an undercover agent to perform the most daring rescue of all time. Before the foundation of the world our Lord knew He was to be a 007 agent, coming secretly, clandestinely, incognito to comprehensively—and at the same time—both defeat the devil and win the hearts of you and me, his eternal bride! Who would suspect a blue collar, itinerant Rabbi to be capable of such a feat? Before looking at the return of this amazing Bridegroom, we will first look at the people in the Old Covenant who personified bridal love.

Although the bride of the Son of God has to be a very special person, paradoxically *"whoever will"* may qualify. The Lord Jesus Himself does not look for the bride, rather He sends the Holy Spirit to search her out. In this next section, we will look at those who exemplify the sacrificial love and service to others that so captivates the heart of our Saviour.

We see fifteen-year-old Rebekah serving a weary stranger and watering his ten thirsty camels — a truly heroic task. We then will see Ruth, bereaved, barren and broke, caring for her embittered mother-in-law. We will enter into the pain of David, the seemingly unwanted and neglected son, and then we marvel at the grace of God in the life of Bathsheba, grace which enabled her to forgive the king who took her by force, murdered her husband, and was responsible for the death of her first son, a child conceived through rape. We see the pain, the betrayal, the breakthrough to forgiveness and its huge reward. Finally we investigate the life of a feisty teenager who saved an entire nation from extermination.

PART TWO
Types and Shadows

2
Rebekah, the Willing Bride

"They called Rebekah and said to her, 'Will you go with this man?' And she said, 'I will go.'"
(Genesis 24:58)

In the story of Isaac and Rebekah, Isaac is *this man,* and you are Rebekah! What, me? Surely not me, I'm male, I'm definitely not pure, I'm not even a virgin. Or perhaps you may say, I'm divorced, widowed, married already. But no matter your gender, race, or background, the Holy Spirit is after you.

Remember, salvation is a love story. It's also the great rescue plan. In the paradise garden, Adam and Eve comprehensively blew it. With one short subtle temptation, the rule, authority, and dominion granted to them by the Father was passed from them to the Tempter. Freedom and holiness were changed to slavery and sin. But let's look at God's rescue plan as set out in Genesis 24. Though the narrative is about Rebekah, it is also your story.

> "Now Abraham was old, (actually 140 years old) and the Lord had blessed Abraham in all things." (Genesis 24:1)

Abraham mandated the chief of his household staff, Eliezer, to take the long and dangerous journey back from Hebron to Nahor (modern day Iraq) to find a wife for his beloved son, Isaac. Eliezer was to swear an oath that he would not bring back just any wife. Specific instructions were given:

- She should be a worshiper of the One True God.
- She must be a virgin.
- She must be willing to leave her parents, her home, her culture, and friends to take a five-hundred-mile journey back to Hebron to marry a man she had never met—a very difficult camel ride!

The servant added his own stipulation: she must be kind enough to water his camels; all ten of them. Where to find such an amazing bride? Eliezer headed straight for the well outside the town. This was where the young maidens would congregate early mornings and evenings to draw out, not only water, but all the latest gossip.

As the thirsty camels knelt by the well, Eliezer prayed an audacious prayer, *"When I approach a young woman to ask for a drink, let her offer to water my camels also. If she agrees, then I will know that she is the chosen bride for Isaac."*

"Before he had finished speaking Rebekah, came out with her pitcher on her shoulder. Eliezer ran to meet her." (Genesis 24;17)

She was stunningly beautiful, a virgin, and extremely kind and courteous. Not only did she offer refreshment to Eliezer, but she said, *"I will draw water for your camels also, until they have finished drinking."*

Little did Rebekah know that those camels were laden with gifts for her and her family. Little did Eliezer know that Rebekah was the granddaughter of Abraham's brother,

Rebekah, the Willing Bride

Nahor. It was only after she had finished the Herculean task, that the servant brought out gifts of gold weighing ten shekels. On learning her identity, the servant bowed and worshipped God.

More running! The astonished Rebekah RAN back home with the news of a stranger's visit. Her brother, Laban ran out to meet Abraham's emissary. Imagine the excitement as Eliezer explained his mission and unloaded ten camel's worth of *"jewelry of silver, jewelry of gold, clothing and precious treasures."*

Now for the crunch; the moment of truth. This man has appeared out of the blue. Now he is asking you to leave everything loved and familiar, to take a bumpy, six-week journey to marry a man you have never met; to love this man extravagantly, to entrust your entire life and future to him. What would YOU say? (Remember, we said, "You are Rebekah.")

For Rebekah it looked like a big ask. She had little knowledge of her would-be-bridegroom; only what the servant had told her. Yet, at age of perhaps fifteen, she simply says, "I will go."

Many weeks later Isaac is meditating in the countryside when he spots the camel train bearing his bride... *"Then Isaac took Rebekah, and she became his wife, and he loved her."* Rebekah received many gifts from the father of her bridegroom—gold, silver, precious stones, and garments. She knew nothing of the real bride price Isaac had secretly paid for her. We will discover this later, for marriage is a sharing of intimate secrets.

God is not mocked, neither is He defeated. His plan for children and a bride did not change. It went underground. So now in the daily detritus of modern life, the Holy Spirit comes searching, wooing, whispering. He is after you. He is after me. What is His aim? A bride for the Son. The Holy Spirit knows there is no one commensurate with the Son: *"There is none righteous. No not one."*[8]

As the servant journeyed towards Rebekah, full of eager expectation, so the Holy Spirit searches for you. For the servant is none other than an Ambassador sent by the Father to choose a bride for the Son of His love. You are that bride. With what longing the Holy Spirit searches us out! He runs to us loaded with gifts. He knows very well that you and I are not worthy; for we are soaked in sin. He knows that we cannot help ourselves, but He is the Great Helper. Gently He woos us. He entices us. We begin to feel the vacuum; the need for something, someone Other. Little by little He draws us to the Father. Step by step he leads us until we come face to face with our own wickedness, our own mortality. Perhaps we become afraid, for this God is a Consuming Fire. Little by little our eyes are opened. We begin to see the Heavenly Bridegroom.

Then the Holy Spirit whispers, "Will you go with this Man? Will everything and everyone you hold dear become secondary to this consuming love?"

"But I don't really know Him. I only know about Him. How can I trust Him? Life with this Consuming Fire might be difficult, challenging, and even arduous. It will be a giant leap into the unknown."

"Indeed, it will be an adventure, even a hazardous one, but if you dare say to say, 'Yes' to this Man, I will be alongside as your Guide and your Helper."

So, the question is, "Will you go with this Man?" Will you make a lifelong commitment to love Him, serve Him, honour, and obey Him? Will you forsake everything to follow the Lord?

Jesus said, "If anyone desires to come after Me, let him deny himself, and take up his cross daily, and follow Me. For whoever desires to save his life will lose it, but whoever loses his life for My sake will save it. For what profit is it to a man if he gains the whole world, and he himself is destroyed or lost? For whoever is ashamed of Me and My words, of him the Son of Man will be ashamed when He comes in His own glory, and His Father's and of the holy angels." (Luke 9:23-26)

So, **will you go with this Man?**

3

Ruth, the Servant Bride

Ruth said, "Entreat me not to leave you, or to turn back from following after you." (Ruth 1:16)

Three broken women stand at the crossroads. Two are young Moabite widows; the third their widowed mother-in-law, a Jewess. They are on the border of Moab and Naomi has elected to return to her native land of Israel. It's decision time. Will the young women step out into the unknown with Naomi to the land where the true God is worshipped, or will they return to their own people and to their heathen gods?

The Moabites were idol worshippers. They served the god Moloch. Moloch is an angry god. He demands child sacrifice. It is quite possible that Ruth had watched one of her own siblings being burnt alive. Whatever happened in Ruth's childhood it had sickened her. She compared the worship of Moloch to the worship of her deceased Jewish husband and his family and chose the GOD, Y-HW-H, Yahweh.

We read that Orpah kissed Naomi and returned back home. But Ruth "clung" to her mother-in-law. The word clung in Hebrew is "dabaq." It means "to be joined to, cleave to, to be glued together, to be attached, devoted to." It's a very strong word. It is the word used in the marriage ceremony when the minister asks the bride if she is willing, "to forsake all others and keep (cleave to) thee only unto him, as long as ye both shall live."[9] The same question is put to the groom. It is a lifelong commitment of love, honour, and fidelity.

The modern-day marriage service is based on the very first wedding, the one conducted by Father God between Adam and Eve.

"Therefore a man shall leave his father and mother and be 'dabaq' to his wife, and they shall become one flesh." (Genesis 2:24)

Ruth "clings" to Naomi and says,

"Entreat me not to leave you, or turn back from following you; for wherever you go, I will go; and wherever you lodge, I will lodge. Your people shall be my people, and your God, my God. Where you die, I will die and there will I be buried." (Ruth 1:16)

She then seals it with an oath:

"The Lord so do to me and more also if anything but death separates you and me." (v.17)

The watching angels stand in awe while to the Father and Son, the Holy Spirit whispers, "We have found a bride."

Covenant Commitment

When Ruth uttered these amazing words to a broken and bitter Naomi, she was making a covenant commitment. Not only was she giving herself to Naomi, but she was also giving herself to Naomi's God — Yahweh. I believe as these words were uttered; all heaven applauded. So that Naomi could understand the depth of her commitment, Ruth sealed it with an oath. She virtually said, "May God strike me dead if anything but death separates me from you."

When Christians marry today, we still vow to love and cherish each other "until death do us part."

What Ruth was demonstrating here was total intimacy. "I will be with you day and night. I will never leave you. I choose you over my biological parents and their gods. When I married your son, I became part of *your* family. I am committed *to you*. Whatever hardship you face, Naomi, I'm here to face it with you. I will love and protect you all your days."

Ruth was highly motivated. Living with this Hebrew family had kindled within her a deep desire to know and worship the One True God, El Shaddai–the Almighty; the One who is more than enough. It was noted in heaven for, *"The eyes of the Lord run to and fro throughout the whole earth, to show Himself strong on behalf of those whose heart is loyal to Him."* (2 Chronicles 16:9)

Fulfilling the Vow

The reality of the situation hit when Naomi and Ruth finally arrived in Bethlehem to a neglected shell of a house devoid of comfort, and crucially, food. In the midst of this unmitigated trauma Ruth stands out like a bright and shining light. Notwithstanding Naomi's mental state, or maybe because of it, Ruth purposed to continue loving and supporting her. At some personal risk (foreigners were fair game for predators), Ruth decided to walk to the nearest barley field to pick up the leftovers from the harvesters. For long months, Ruth toils in the heat, picking up scraps of barley and later wheat. When she returns home, her work is not finished. The grains need to be ground into flour and then baked to become bread. Love and hunger are good motivators!

But someone was watching. As God would have it, the field chosen by Ruth belonged to Boaz, a wealthy landowner. Ruth does not know it, but this is none other than the leader of the tribe of Judah.[10] Little does she realize that one day soon she will be married to the owner of this field. He appears on her very first day in time for the lunch break and straight away something about Ruth's demeanor captivates him. He speaks kindly to her, shares his lunch with her, and orders his young men not to touch her. It would seem that Boaz was a widower. He too is childless.

Although he is initially attracted to Ruth, Boaz puts these thoughts out of his mind. After all, she a foreigner, a former idol worshiper, and she is much younger than him. When Ruth returns home after a day of backbreaking reaping, she is greatly comforted. It is a long time since anyone has been kind to her. But now someone has protected her, someone has been compassionate; so much so that she returns home carrying thirty pounds of barley. As they take supper together every evening, Naomi questions her daughter about her day. It soon becomes apparent that Boaz is showing Ruth unusual favor; more pertinently Boaz is not just a wealthy landowner, he is a close relative.

Four backbreaking months pass. Naomi and Ruth had arrived at the beginning of the barley harvest, usually March or April. It is now June, the beginning of the wheat harvest. Day in and day out Ruth has faithfully risen early and made the trek to the fields, toiling in the heat of the day.

Taking pity on her weary daughter-in-law, Naomi hatches an audacious plan!

The Levirate Law & the Kinsman Redeemer

Realizing that both Boaz and Ruth are lonely and bereaved, Naomi remembers the edict given by God through Moses called 'the Levirate Law.'[11] This is the law of the brother-in-law. Essentially, this law decrees if a man dies with no offspring, then his brother should take the widow as his wife. The first son of that marriage would be considered to be the son of the dead man and the child born would inherit his property. Mahlon's brother, Chilion, had also died so could not fulfill that role, but Boaz was a cousin to Naomi's husband, Elimelech. Not only did the Kinsman Redeemer have to raise up a son to inherit the dead man's property, but he first had to buy back that property. Something else too – if the dead man had been murdered, then the Kinsman Redeemer becomes the Avenger of Blood. He is obligated to pursue the killer and put him to death. Mahlon died of natural causes so fortunately for Boaz, there is no one to be avenged. But as we shall see later, our Lord and Saviour, Jesus is the ultimate Kinsman Redeemer.

It seems that Boaz needs a prod, so Naomi instructs Ruth on the proposal protocol. Ruth is to take a bath, anoint herself, and put on her finest clothing. Then she is to go secretly to the threshing floor where Boaz will be supervising the winnowing when the grains of wheat are extracted from the husk. Ruth is to wait until Boaz sleeps. Then she is to creep in secretly and lie at his feet, covering herself with the edge of his robe. (This is such an exciting love story!) At midnight Boaz awakes and is astonished to find a woman at his feet.

"Who are you?" he whispers.

"I am Ruth, your maidservant. Take me under your wing, cover me with the edge of your garment, for you are my kinsman redeemer."[12] Wow! I think this is the only female proposal of marriage recorded in the Bible. Boaz stands, lifts her up, and covers her with his mantle. Now he is the one proposing. A covering is a protection. It is a part of the covenant, a symbol of lifelong preservation from the groom to his bride. The prophet Isaiah knew this as he excitedly proclaims:

"I will greatly rejoice in the Lord, my soul shall be joyful in her God: for He has clothed me with the garments of salvation. He has covered me with the robe of righteousness." (61:10)

Astonishment turns to delight and suddenly Boaz can't wait. By morning, he is at Bethlehem's gate along with ten city elders requesting that Ruth, the Moabite widow of Mahlon, be given to him to fulfill the Levirate Law of progeny. A marriage is quickly arranged and all the people at the gate and all the elders pour out their blessings:

"May you prosper and be famous in Bethlehem. May your house be like the house of Perez, whom Tamar bore to Judah." (Ruth 4:12)

These prayers were abundantly answered. It is interesting that the commitment and vow Ruth made to Naomi in chapter one was replicated in chapter four, when Boaz made his marriage vow to Ruth. Boaz made his commitment before the elders of Bethlehem at 'the gate,' the place where legal transactions were carried out. What we have here is an example of 'sowing and reaping,' almost literally. Just a few months after Ruth committed herself to Naomi, Boaz was to make a lifelong commitment to Ruth in the presence of many witnesses. Let's look at the tremendous blessings of this union:

Blessings for Ruth and Naomi

- Mourning has turned to joy.
- The hungry are full.
- Poverty has been turned into wealth.
- The outcast is brought in.
- The barren has become fruitful.
- Naomi, once bitter is sweet. She is *"restored and nourished."*
- The entire population of Bethlehem rejoices.

These are the blessings we too receive as the bride of Christ.

Blessings for Boaz

- He gains a beautiful young wife.
- He fathers Obed
- Obed begets Jesse who in turn fathers David, the greatest king of Israel.
- Subsequently every king of Judah is descended through the royal line of David.

- Twenty-eight generations after David, King Jesus is born.

Blessings for the King of the Universe

Little did Ruth know when she left the known for the unknown that the fields where she was reaping would one day become her fields and that she, the barren gentile widow, would become great in the Kingdom of God.

The last verse of Judges has this sad commentary, *"In those days there was no king in Israel, every man did what was right in his own eyes."* So there was chaos and anarchy. But when God rewards, He rewards abundantly. It would seem that Ruth quickly conceived a son, Obed 'worshiper of God.' How wonderful that a former worshiper of Molech could give birth to a worshiper of the one true God! Obed became the father of Jesse, who fathered eight sons and two daughters. The lastborn son was David, *"a man after God's own heart."*

In His love and His mercy, our God allowed Ruth to become the great grandmother of Israel's most famous king; a king boasted of in heaven; a king of whom our Lord and Savior, Jesus Christ proclaims Himself to be, *"of the root and offspring of David."* (Revelation 22:14) Before Ruth, there was anarchy in Israel, but thanks to her obedience and the redeeming love of Boaz, their union was, in time, to bring forth the greatest king who has ever lived. In the short-term, anarchy was replaced by godly government. And as we will discover when we look at the life of King David, we will find him to be a type of the worshiping bride and a bride who is a warrior.

The Depth of Ruth's Commitment

- She left everything to follow Naomi — her parents, siblings, friends, country, gods, and security. She stepped into the unknown.
- Every day for many months she labored from early morning until late evening to provide food for her mother-in-law. The work was backbreaking and dangerous.
- What Ruth was demonstrating here was total intimacy. "I will be with you day and night. I choose you over my biological parents, for when I married your son, I became part of your family. I will never leave you. I am committed to you, (Naomi) on this journey; together we will face poverty and hardship. Whatever comes, I'll be at your side.

What was Ruth's Motivation?

- Love for Naomi.
- Love and devotion to Naomi's God, Yahweh.

The Lord Jesus Christ is our Heavenly Bridegroom. He loves us with a passion that perhaps we cannot fully comprehend until we see Him face to face. The Holy Spirit woos us and draws our hearts to Jesus. We only glimpse Him dimly but deep down we know we need to make a decision. Will we step into the unknown like Ruth? Will we follow Him wherever He leads? Will we love Him with all our heart, all our soul, and all our strength? Will we forsake all 'others' — legitimate pursuits, earthly pleasures, every idol, fame, and fortune to love and serve Him?

We can learn a lot from Ruth. The vow she made to Naomi was costly. The daily toil was both dirty and debasing. She served gladly, motivated by love. Let us not be like Orpah and turn back.

Rewards for Her Devotion

- Ruth made a covenant with Naomi.
- Boaz made a covenant with Ruth.
- God made a covenant with Ruth and Boaz.

Our Heavenly Bridegroom laid down His life for us. That is the extent of His agape love for us. If we are to be a bride commensurate with Him, we too need to lay down our lives for Him. We need to leave everything, yes, everything for Him. He is preeminent. Everything else is secondary. Yes, we need to give our hearts, our love, our service, and our devotion. But perhaps more than anything at this time of trial, we need to give Him our time. This is a season full of challenges, but let's sit at His feet, hunger for His Word, and give Him our utter devotion. Let's not be like Orpah who turned back.

Ruth's vow to Naomi epitomizes the first and second bridal commandments:

> "You shall love the Lord your God with all your heart, with all your soul and with all your strength. You shall love your neighbor as yourself." (Luke 10:27)

We should not forget this tender lyrical narrative is essentially a LOVE STORY. It is the deep covenantal love of a sorrowing daughter for her broken mother-in-law. Gentile Ruth puts aside her own grief to lay down her life for Naomi. All heaven watches and links her to a lonely Israelite; Boaz. The two become one and the One New Man is born. How beautiful that our Messiah is descended from both Jew and Gentile!

Perhaps we can say with Ruth:

"I will not leave You or turn back from following You. Where You go, I will go. Your people (the body and bride of Christ) shall be my people. I will serve You all my days and this is my covenant with You."

Will you 'dabaq' to Jesus?

4
David, the Worshiping Bride

We meet several outstanding men and women on our journey through Scripture: people like Abraham, the friend of God; Isaac, the perfect son; Rebekah the willing bride; and Boaz, the Kinsman Redeemer. We could also mention Enoch, "who walked with God," and Moses, the outstanding intercessor who "spoke with God face to face."

But among even the greatest in Scripture stands David. Perhaps more than anyone he typifies the bride of Christ, for the true bride is firstly a worshiper, and worship leads to warfare. David surely exemplifies both these qualities. This man is so beloved that God calls him, *"a man after My own heart."* The Bible speaks of him more than any other character. Sixty chapters are devoted to him in the Old Testament. He is mentioned twenty-three times in the New, culminating in Revelation 22:17 where the triumphal Lord Jesus proclaims Himself to be *"of the root and offspring of David."*

The Discarded Son

Like his great grandmother, Ruth, David did not have the best start in life. It is almost as if he was a neglected child. He was probably the tenth child of the family, coming after seven strapping brothers and two feisty sisters. Sadly, it would seem that he had little value. He was sent out of the family home at an early age to take care of his father's sheep. Certainly, this was a lonely occupation, and dangerous too. (Witness his encounters with a lion and a bear.) Why was not an older brother sent with him? And why, when the great prophet Samuel came to town specifically requesting the pleasure of the company of the entire Jesse household, was David left behind? He was valueless to his biological father, but his Heavenly Father who "sees all things" loved and highly valued him.

What made David so attractive to Almighty God? (Oh, my heart leaps!) It was worship, and worship was the very foundation of David's life. As Jesus proclaimed to the Samaritan woman,

> "True worshipers will worship the Father in spirit and in truth. The Father is seeking such to worship Him. God is Spirit and those who worship Him must worship in spirit and in truth." (John 4:23)

Yes, God is actively searching out those who will worship and value Him.

> "The eyes of the Lord run to and fro throughout the earth to show Himself strong on behalf of those whose heart is loyal to Him." (2 Chronicles 16:9)

There on the lonely hillside, the teenage David gazing into the nightly sky, learned to worship his heavenly Father. It would seem that David with his homemade harp began composing hymns of praise to his Maker at that time. Altogether, he composed 73 songs of the 150 given to us in the book of Psalms. Witness Psalm 8. Could it have been written when he was just a teen?

"O Lord, our Lord, how excellent is Your Name in all the earth, who have set your glory above the heavens! Out of the mouths of babes and nursing infants You have ordained praise... When I consider Your heavens, the work of Your fingers, the moon, and the stars, which You have ordained, what is man that You are mindful of him and the son of man that You visit him?"

Perhaps Psalm 9 verses 1 & 2 sum up the very essence of the man:

"I will praise You, O Lord, with my whole heart; I will tell of Your marvelous works. I will rejoice and be glad and rejoice in You; I will sing praise to Your Name, O Most High."

On that Judean hillside, while nightly contemplating the heavens, David glimpsed the magnificent glory and greatness of God. How could he know that Almighty God counts each star and calls them all by name?[13] It is past finding out, for they are innumerable. In our own galaxy — the Milky Way — there are billions of stars, and among them Planet Earth looks like a tiny dot. And yet we are told that there are hundreds of billions of galaxies and that the universe is continually being created. This is the magnificent, incomprehensible Being who called David by name and revealed His greatness and glory to a lonely boy away from home.

The Much-Loved Son

David was loved by God! What an epithet! How would you like to be called, *"a man after God's own heart"*? Even later in life when he sinned in such an appalling way, after his wholehearted repentance, those terrible crimes were blotted out and he was still *"a man after God's own heart."* (Acts 13:22) And when the Christ child was born in Bethlehem of Judea, that birthplace was chosen because both Joseph, the stepfather and Mary, the birth mother, *"were of the house and lineage of David."* This was the fulfillment of the promise made to King David by God through the prophet Nathan that through David's seed God would establish an everlasting kingdom. A promise fulfilled with the birth of the Messiah, "great David's greater Son."

For David, worship led to warfare. In fact, worship was his secret weapon, as we see in Psalm 27. Here we find him, still a teenager, but the anointed King of Israel; anointed, running for his life. We find him hiding in a cave surrounded by perhaps three thousand of Saul's men. What does he do? He ignores the strife, the tumult, and the danger and begins to worship God. He is totally alone. His father and mother have forsaken him. The reigning King, to whom he is utterly loyal, is trying to take his life. But here in the cave, David sets out the game plan of his life:

> **"One thing** have I desired of the Lord, that will I seek: that I may dwell in the house of the Lord all the days of my life, to behold the beauty of the Lord and to inquire in His temple. For in the time of trouble He shall hide me in his pavilion, in the secret place of His tabernacle He shall hide me. And now my head shall

be lifted up above my enemies all around me. Therefore I will offer sacrifices of joy in His tabernacle; I will sing, yes, I will sing praises to the Lord." (Psalm 27:4-6)

Yes, praise works; David discounted the army surrounding him and the fact that there was no escape. Praise and worship allow God to fight our battles for us. As David worshiped while his life was threatened, the Philistines invaded Judah and Saul called his armies off. David's life was spared yet again.

The Man of One Thing

God is looking for people of One Thing. He found such a one in Mary, the sister of Martha who sat at the feet of Jesus drinking in His every word. Mary so loved Jesus that she took her bridal anointing oil worth a year's wages and poured it over her Lord, anointing him for his burial. Jesus said of her,

> "**One thing** is needed, and Mary has chosen that good part which will not be taken away from her." (Luke 10:39, 42)

The Apostle Paul was such a man:

> "**One thing** I do... I press towards the goal for the prize of the upward call of God in Christ Jesus." (Philippians 4:13, 14)

Yes, God seeks those who will worship Him fervently with all their hearts. David's 'One Thing' desire was to live continually in the reverential awe of the Presence of God.

The Extravagant Worshiper

David was an extravagant worshiper. This is exemplified when he brought the Ark of the Covenant back to Jerusalem. For King David, this was the zenith of his achievements for the Ark represented the very Presence of the Only True God. Before the Ark could be properly housed, David had first to defeat all Israel's enemies and capture Jerusalem, the city of God. When the scene was set, he summoned all Israel to be there. It was a party and what a party! There were 870 musicians playing harps and cymbals, castanets, strings, and trumpets. The priests added to the excitement with their noisy shofars, an exuberant cacophony. All the army captains and thousands of troops were there. In fact, all of Israel was invited to celebrate their God on that day. (1 Chronicles 15)

King David led the procession, dancing exuberantly before The Presence with all his might. Surprisingly, he did not wear his kingly regalia but a simple robe of fine linen; the very same robe the Levites wore, showing us that like our Lord Jesus Christ, we too are reborn to be both kings and priests.

> [Jesus] "loved us and washed us from our sins in His own blood and has made us kings and priests to His God and Father, to Him be glory and dominion forever and ever." (Revelation 1:6)

King David knew that worship bring us into the very Presence of a Holy God. Our praise and adoration rise like sweet incense before Him. Moreover, as the praise ascends, the Presence descends. Oh, let us be like David, the man after God's own heart learning to worship in times of plenty, times of want, times of abounding, and in times of tribulation.

The Extravagant Giver

When Mary, the sister of Martha poured a pound of costly spikenard over the feet of the Lord Jesus Christ, we are told the cost was an entire years' wages. How much do you earn each year? Well, that is how much it cost her. Every time David was victorious in battle, he came back loaded with spoil. We are told, "*He died in a good old age, full of riches and honor.*" (1 Chronicles 29:28) What did he do with all this wealth? Let's listen to him:

> "Because I have set my affection on the house of my God, I have given to the house of my God... my own special treasure of gold and silver." (1 Chronicles 29:3)

To be precise, he gave for the building of the Temple 113 tons of the best gold and 214 tons of silver. Following the Kings' example, the people now came willingly to give a further 188 tons of gold, 377 tons of silver, 679 tons of bronze and 3,775 tons of iron, in addition to onyx and precious stones. King David had prepared everything needed for the building of Solomon's Temple. Significantly, as he "sat before the Lord," he was given a minutely detailed plan for the dwelling place of the Most High God. No wonder it was one of the wonders of the world.

True worship is not merely giving our money, it means giving ourselves: everything we have, everything we are, and everything we hope to be. It is costly. Witness Abraham, *"I and the lad will go to **worship.**"* Worship? Put to death your beloved son? Yes.

> "I beseech you brethren by the mercies of God that you present your bodies **a living sacrifice**, which is your reasonable worship." (Romans 12:1)

Can we, like David, be the worshiping bride; the people of the One thing?

> "One thing have I desired of the Lord, that will I seek after; that I may dwell in the house of the Lord all the days of my life to behold the beauty of the Lord and to inquire in His temple."

Can we present our bodies to God, together with our hopes, dreams, and aspirations as our reasonable worship?

The Forgiving Worshiper

True worshipers forgive. They forgive themselves and they forgive others. Fifteen times Saul attempted to kill David. On two occasions David had the opportunity to kill Saul. Such was his respect for God that even though he had been anointed king of Israel, he waited for God's timing. More than once he declared, *"God forbid that I should touch the Lord's anointed."*

Not only did David learn to forgive, but there came a time when he needed God's extravagant forgiveness.[14] Sadly, the man after God's own heart sinned comprehensively. We can count, adultery and murder; both of them punishable by death. Add rape, betrayal of a brother officer, forced marriage, and the death of a child conceived in lust to the list. If he sinned extravagantly, his repentance was deep and sincere; seven days of fasting, face down clothed in sackcloth and ashes. Those who have been forgiven much, love much.

As much as David forgave (King Saul, others, himself) perhaps no one in the Old Testament was more forgiving than the next Old Testament saint we will look at: Bathsheba. But first, we need to find out why David was so successful as a worshiper and a mighty warrior.

5
David, the Warrior Bride

When Solomon ascended to throne of Israel, he inherited land that stretched all the way from the River Nile in Egypt to the Euphrates in modern day Syria. It was the largest swathe of land Israel had ever recorded and it was the fulfillment of God's prophecy to Abram in Genesis 15:18. In his forty-year reign, King David never lost a battle. He was indeed a mighty warrior. He comprehensively defeated the Philistines, the Moabites, the Ammonites, the Amalekites, the people of Edom and Aram so that Solomon was able to reign for a further forty years of peace.

What Was The Secret of David's Success?

1. He had an intimate relationship with the Creator of the Universe.

David knew that the God he served was all great, all powerful and in charge.

> "O Lord (my) Lord, How excellent is Your name in all the earth. (You) have set Your glory above the heavens! When I consider Your heavens, the work of Your fingers, the moon and the stars, which You have ordained, what is man that You are mindful of him? Or the son of man that You visit him? For you

have made him a little lower than the angels and You have crowned him with glory and honour." (Psalm 8:1, 3-5)

Here we have an insight into David's heart and mind. As he contemplates the heavenly host, he begins to realize that God is indeed very big, mind bogglingly big. The God of the Universe is awesome in holiness, majestic in power and glory. By comparison, man is puny. But with this magnificent God on his side, David could achieve great things.

David lived literally under an open heaven; night after night a Holy God revealed Himself to this eighth son, so that he could boldly say:

"The heavens declare the glory of God, and the firmament shows His handiwork, and night unto night reveals knowledge. There is no speech or language where their voice is not heard." (Psalm 19: 1-3)

How could David know that stars emit sound and that pulsars praise the Lord? Only recently have scientists discovered this to be true. What scientists have recently discovered through the exploration of space, David knew by revelation. And this was three thousand years ago!

2. David knew God as his Father.

In those solitary years, David sat in God's University. He learned that although he was the biological son of Jesse, his authentic eternal genesis was in the heart of God the Father.

"You formed my inward parts; You covered me in my mother's womb. Your eyes saw my substance being yet unformed and in your book they all were written, the days determined for me when as yet there were none of them. How precious are thoughts to me O God, how great the sum of them. If I could count them, they would be more in number than the sand." (Psalm 139: 13, 15, 16)

Armed with this knowledge, it was a simple matter for young David to finish off a lion and a bear. Equally with such a powerful God as his father, the nine-foot Goliath looked like a puny weakling.

3. Every battle was fought, not in his own strength, but in the strength of the Lord.

David recognized that day and night Almighty God is worshiped by myriads of angels. He knew his God to be The Lord of Hosts, that is The God of the Angel Armies. He never entered a battle in his own strength and that is why he could say to Goliath:

"You come to me with a sword, with a spear, and with a javelin. But I come to you in the name of the Lord of hosts, the God of the armies of Israel, whom you have defiled. This day the Lord will deliver you into my hand… then all this assembly will know that the Lord does not save with sword and spear; for the battle is the Lord's." (1 Samuel 17: 45, 47)

After Goliath, David fought many more battles. He conquered every single enemy. Wherever David went, even on the run, he was accompanied by a priest and often a prophet. He never went to war without first seeking the face of his God for the battle plan. At the lowest point of his life (when Ziklag was burnt and the families of all his men had been captured together with all the spoil they had acquired after six years on the run), we read that David was greatly distressed. But what does he do? Firstly, David strengthened himself in the Lord. Having gained strength and courage, he inquired of the Lord. And this is the refrain that we hear before every battle.

4. David attributed every victory to the Lord, his God.

In Psalm eighteen, (so noteworthy that it is repeated in 2 Samuel 22) David attributes every success to his Heavenly Father. He even claims that God did the fighting:

> "The Lord thundered from heaven, the Most High uttered His voice. He sent out arrows and scattered them; lightning bolts and He vanquished them. God is my strength and power. He makes my way perfect... He teaches my hands to make war, so that my arms can bend a bow of bronze." (2 Sam. 22:14, 15, 33, 35)

And finally two of my favourite verses:

> "For by You I can run against a troop, by my God I can leap over a wall. As for God His way is perfect;

the word of the Lord is proven; He is a shield to all who put their trust in Him." (Psalm 18: 29, 30)

5. David forgave his enemies.

If we think that God's anointing brings automatic joy, peace and victory. We have to think again. Every bride of Christ must learn to endure hardship. Each one of us needs to be tried and tested by affliction. We need "the iron to enter our soul" like Joseph.

> "Joseph was sold as a slave. They hurt his feet with fetters, and he was laid in irons... The word of the Lord tested him." (Psalm 105:17-19)

If we are to rule and reign with Christ and know His resurrection power, we will be required to suffer with Him. All great men and women of God endured disappointment, distress, and hardship. Witness Noah, Abraham, Joseph, Ruth, Paul, and the most brutal humiliation of all, poured upon our Bridegroom King, Jesus.

No wonder everyone loved and admired David the giant-killer! No wonder the maidens sang, *"Saul has slain his thousands and David his ten thousands."* (1 Samuel 18:7) Hearing this chant, King Saul became insanely jealous. He now sees David as a rival. Fifteen times Saul attempts to kill the man who is now his son-in-law.

The hero of Israel flees for his life and for six long years he is on the run; more night vigils under an open heaven. He has been anointed King of Israel, yet the reigning king, Saul, tries to kill him.

How does David respond to these murder attempts? Let us learn: Three times David has the opportunity to kill King Saul. This is his response:

> "The Lord forbid that I should stretch forth my hand against him (Saul), seeing he is the anointed of the Lord." (1 Samuel 24:6)

He repeats the same words when Abishai, David's nephew stands over the sleeping Saul and prepares to kill him. David merely tells Saul,

> "As your life was valued much this day in my eyes, so let my life be valued much in the eyes of the Lord and let Him deliver me out of all tribulation." (1 Samuel 26:24)

As always, David was not looking to man to save him, but to the Lord God.

6. Learning in the School of Suffering.

From solitude to spotlight, God's education for the boy who had captured His heart continued. David has learned to let God fight his battles. After the years of privation, the Lord steps in and fights for him and Saul is killed by the Philistines. David finally graduates and is anointed King of Israel in Hebron.

7. A man after every man's heart.

Not only was David a man after God's own heart, but significantly, as an outstanding leader, he was a man after every man's heart. How else as a fugitive on the run did this very young man turn four hundred distressed, discontented debtors into an elite fighting force?

> "David... escaped to the cave of Adullam... and everyone who was in distress, everyone who was in debt, and everyone who was discontented gathered to him." (1 Samuel 22:1-2)

Such was the strength of his character, and such was the anointing of the Holy Spirit upon him that at the end of his reign, David could count twelve military divisions each containing twenty-four thousand troops: a massive, loyal, and well-disciplined army. Every single one of these men would gladly lay down their lives to protect their warrior king.

Yet before his coronation, these four hundred discontents wanted to stone him. This was when their city of refuge was burned, and their wives and children taken captive by the Amalekites.

> "David was greatly distressed because the people spoke of stoning him... every man grieving for his sons and his daughters." (1 Samuel 30:6)

In this truly dreadful situation, what does David do? Firstly, *"He strengthened himself in the Lord his God."* Then *"he inquired of the Lord"* through Abiathar, the priest, asking for directions. The Lord gives both strength and direction with these wonderful words:

"Pursue, for you shall surely overtake and without fail recover all." (1 Samuel 30:4-8)

It's nightfall and the men have been marching for three days. But by the power of their God and godly leadership, they are strengthened to march on through the night. As the Holy Spirit leads them, they discover the Amalakites...

"Eating, drinking, and dancing because of the great spoil they had taken from the Philistines and from the land of Judah. Then David attacked them from twilight until the next evening... David recovered all." (1 Samuel 30:16-19)

This is a wonderful example of the Lord's strength being made perfect in human weakness. They returned not only with every wife and child, not only with all their stolen possessions, but with masses of spoil that the Amalekites had taken both from Philistine and Judah. They were loaded.

While David and his men were pursuing the Amalekites, King Achish defeated Saul and shortly after, David moved to Hebron where he was crowned king of Judah.

Whatever plunder David took from enemy camps, he dedicated to the Lord; so much so that when he was about to die, he could say to Solomon, "I have prepared with all my might gold, silver, bronze, wood, onyx and marble." (1 Chronicles 29:2) His own personal offering was a staggering five thousand tons of gold in addition to silver and precious stones.

8. David never went into battle without first seeking God's face for the battle plan.

David's wilderness experience was to last for six years before he was crowned King over Judah. It took another seven years before he became king over all Israel. He waited until the northern tribes invited him. Under his leadership, the entire country was united. Through good times and bad, David was never without a priest and later a prophet. He surrounded himself with godly counselors. But in the battles he fought, he never failed to seek God's face and hear His voice for the battle plan. As we have read, "David inquired of the Lord," this was his habitual stance. Indeed those who trust in the Lord shall never be put to shame.

Perhaps His greatest victory was the capture of Jerusalem. Again, it was the Lord who gave him the strategy: to climb up clandestinely by way of the water shaft. After this stunning victory, we read: *"So David went on and became great and the Lord of Hosts was with him."* (2 Samuel 5:10)

At the end of his forty-year reign, David the Warrior King had successfully defeated all of Israel's enemies. The territory of Israel had increased tenfold, from six thousand square miles to sixty thousand square miles. The ark was safely in Jerusalem and the priests and Levites had been organized into twenty-four divisions so that worship, praise, and prophecy could ascend to the Throne Room of the Eternal God unceasingly day and night. There were twelve military divisions each boasting twenty-four thousand troops.

We can learn so much from Israel's greatest king. We too can achieve great victories as we, like David, understand that a major and effective strategy of warfare is worship.

6
Bathsheba, The Forgiving Bride

One fateful evening, a young bride named Bathsheba took a ritual cleansing bath after her menstrual flow according to the Jewish custom.[15] This young lady was stunningly beautiful. As we shall see, her beauty was not only external, but we find a deep inner beauty rooted in her faith in Yahweh. She was probably about seventeen years old and newly married.

Bathsheba was not only beautiful but high born. Her grandfather was Ahitophel, King David's Counsellor. Her father, Eliam[16] (like her husband, Uriah) was one of King David's 'mighty men.' These men were warriors of the King's elite force, comprising of just thirty men: men renowned both for their bravery on the battlefield, but also for their personal piety. It would seem that Bathsheba had everything going for her until one disastrous night.

It was a time of war, the Israelites were stationed on the battlefield besieging Rabbah, the capital of Ammon. Uriah was there, as was his father-in-law, Eliam. It was assumed that their leader, King David was with them for it was he who always led his troops into battle. So when that spring evening Bathsheba was summoned to the palace, she must have been very surprised. What she did not know was that her ritual bath and her naked body had been observed, and observed by none other than the king. Seeing her, his heart was inflamed with lust and desire.

To be tempted is one thing; to give into the temptation will lead to severe consequences. Consider this: King David was a married man. In fact he had many wives[17] right there with him in the palace, not to mention several concubines. Secondly, when he inquired, "Who is this girl?" he was clearly told, "She is Bathsheba. Her father is Eliam. Her husband is Uriah."

Both Eliam and Uriah are his loyal troops and David knew full well that the father of Eliam is Ahitophel, his wise and trusted counselor. STOP, DAVID! RED LIGHTS, DAVID! RED LIGHTS! David now knows the identity of his victim but recklessly chooses to take no notice of the warning. His response; *"Send for her."* She was sent for, and he took her. Having satisfied himself he now sends her away like a common street woman.

Many commentators see Bathsheba as a scheming seductress, but as we read the Scripture carefully, we discover that nothing is further from the truth. But first let's look at the consequences: It is amazing that after this illicit 'one night stand' David, the man after God's heart seems conscience hardened. He blindly goes from one grave sin to another. Adultery was punishable by stoning. By taking Bathsheba, David puts not only her life at risk but that his own life, too. He did not consider that his actions might result in a pregnancy but that is exactly what happened. He gets a message, *"I am with child."*

For David this is very bad news. Uriah has been away fighting, so he cannot be the father. If the news gets out, it could be a death sentence for both of them. What to do?

One sin leads to another. 'Send for Uriah. If Uriah sleeps with his wife, it's not too late to pass the child off as his.' Good try David but Uriah is a man of principle; his name means, 'The Lord is my light.'

His response, *"The Ark of Israel... my lord Joab and all the troops are encamped in the open fields. Shall I then go to my house, eat and drink and lie with my wife? As you live and your soul lives, I will not do this thing."*

Nonplussed David tries again. He plies Uriah with alcohol until he is drunk. But even in that befuddled state, Uriah will not betray his warrior mates. Little does Uriah know that this seals his doom. David sends him back to Rabbah carrying his own death warrant. Joab arranges for Uriah to be on the frontlines in the place of extreme danger. Worse still, David tells Joab to withdraw all the soldiers. Betrayed and alone, Uriah is killed.

It gets worse. Bathsheba is allowed seven days to grieve for her husband. She is then summoned once more to the palace, this time to become wife number nineteen. David relaxes now. Hopefully this child can be passed off as a legitimate child of the new marriage; a child who just came early.

Let's take an inventory, David: firstly the rape of a colleague's wife, a virtuous young lady who is the daughter of another loyal soldier. And not only that, but she is also the beloved granddaughter of the man closest to you, Ahitophel. Add the betrayal and murder of your new wife's husband. Not only that David, but you also put Bathsheba's life on the line, and your own life too. The pregnancy progresses and nine months after the rape, a son is born; a beautiful baby, who lives only a few months.

Nemesis is coming. God is not mocked. We now read, *"But the thing that David had done displeased the Lord."* Note it is David who stands condemned, not Bathsheba.[18] Nemesis comes in the shape of the prophet Nathan. It takes a brave man to confront a powerful king with his sins. But Nathan pulls no punches...

"Thou art the man... Why have you despised the commandment of the Lord to do evil in His sight? You have killed Uriah with the sword; you have taken his wife to be your wife."

Then the consequences:

"I will raise up adversity against you from your own house; I will take your wives... and give them to your neighbor, and he shall lie with your wives... for you did it secretly but I will do it openly. The child who is born to you shall surely die."

Grave sins, David. Grave effects. So it was that the child conceived by rape sickens and dies. This is just the beginning of David's sorrows. Firstly the baby dies, then follows the rape of Tamar, David's daughter by her half-brother, Ammon. This in turn leads to the murder of Ammon by Absalom, brother of Tamar.
Worse is to come. Absalom, enraged by David's earlier refusal to punish Ammon, effects a coup against his father and is joined by a distressed Ahitophel. The coup fails. Absalom is killed and Ahitophel commits suicide. All this in spite of David's deep repentance. It is salutary to note that, *"If we confess our sins God is faithful and just to forgive us our sins and to cleanse us from all unrighteousness."* (1 John 1:9) Wonderfully, we are not only cleansed, not only forgiven, but on confession, our sins are actually erased from our record and from God's memory. They are cast *"as far as the east is from the west,"* never to be remembered. (Psalm 103:12) We are forgiven but we, like David, must bear the consequences.

How deep was King David's repentance? Firstly he lay prostrate on the ground in sackcloth and ashes, fasting and pleading with his Father to allow Bathsheba's child to live. He was truly penitent. For seven days and nights he pleaded for mercy. On the seventh day the child died, but during that time David was comforted by the revelation that the child would live in God's Kingdom and that one day, the child, his mother and King David himself would be reunited in the Kingdom to come.

David paid a heavy price for his horrendous crimes, but when faced with his sins, his repentance was correspondingly wholehearted. We have at least two accounts of his cries to God, in Psalms 32 and 51. I love it that though he sinned so appallingly, his repentance gained complete restoration. He is now justified — just as if he had never sinned. He is today still *'a man after God's own heart.'* That gives hope and joy for all of us and impels to quick and wholehearted repentance.

Bathsheba, on the other hand, was innocent yet suffered greatly. Let's take another inventory of the distress:

One. Shock:
King David was everyone's hero; the shepherd boy who slew the giant; the warrior king who fearlessly defeated every foe. The one who, with Joab, took the impregnable city of Jerusalem and made it his capital. This was the king of extravagant worship who jettisoned his kingly robes and danced as a Levite before the Ark of the Lord. How then could such a hero, such a 'man of God' take his brother officer's young wife by force? At the time of this incident David must have been at least forty-three, probably twenty-five years her senior.

Two. Defilement, shame, and ignominy:
As we read through the accounts of David's reign and on through Proverbs, we discover that Bathsheba was an honourable and godly woman. So to be taken and disgraced in such a manner would have caused huge emotional and physical distress.

Three. Outrage. A forced marriage:
With Uriah, Bathsheba had been the only wife. Now she is simply taken to be 'just an extra' wife; one of many. Women had very few rights in those days. She had no choice but to acquiesce. As we have seen, her husband Uriah was a deeply honourable God-fearing man. As such he had a wife who was equal to him. This young couple must have been deeply in love. Now the shock of the rape is compounded by the shock of pregnancy, the fear of stoning, and then the death of her beloved husband.

Four. Mental and emotional distress:
In pregnancy a woman's emotions are heightened as her hormones kick in. Little things can easily upset her. Imagine the sequence: rape, pregnancy, murder compounded by a forced marriage, all happening within the space of two months.

Five. A second death:
Pregnancy is usually a very tender time. There is a baby growing inside you! It is both wonderful and challenging. Suddenly all your attention, all your aspirations are focused on this child. The sickness and discomfort you can bear because of the wonder of childbirth. After such grief and trauma Bathsheba must have drawn comfort from the child

house, eat and drink and lie with my wife? As you live and your soul lives, I will not do this thing."

Nonplussed David tries again. He plies Uriah with alcohol until he is drunk. But even in that befuddled state, Uriah will not betray his warrior mates. Little does Uriah know that this seals his doom. David sends him back to Rabbah carrying his own death warrant. Joab arranges for Uriah to be on the frontlines in the place of extreme danger. Worse still, David tells Joab to withdraw all the soldiers. Betrayed and alone, Uriah is killed.

It gets worse. Bathsheba is allowed seven days to grieve for her husband. She is then summoned once more to the palace, this time to become wife number nineteen. David relaxes now. Hopefully this child can be passed off as a legitimate child of the new marriage; a child who just came early.

Let's take an inventory, David: firstly the rape of a colleague's wife, a virtuous young lady who is the daughter of another loyal soldier. And not only that, but she is also the beloved granddaughter of the man closest to you, Ahitophel. Add the betrayal and murder of your new wife's husband. Not only that David, but you also put Bathsheba's life on the line, and your own life too. The pregnancy progresses and nine months after the rape, a son is born; a beautiful baby, who lives only a few months.

Nemesis is coming. God is not mocked. We now read, *"But the thing that David had done displeased the Lord."* Note it is David who stands condemned, not Bathsheba.[18] Nemesis comes in the shape of the prophet Nathan. It takes a brave man to confront a powerful king with his sins. But Nathan pulls no punches...

wife of his dreams and indeed the godly wife who eclipsed all others. Witness this, Solomon speaking of his childhood:

> "When I was my father's son, tender and the only one in the sight of my mother; he also taught me and said to me: 'Let your heart retain my words; keep my commandments, and live. Get wisdom! Get understanding! Do not forsake her, and she will preserve you.'" (Proverbs 4:4, 5)

And this:

> "Hear the instruction of your father, do not forsake the law of your mother; for they will be a graceful ornament on your head." (Solomon speaking in Proverbs 1:8)

Here we have a scene of domestic harmony: a loving daddy, a loving and wise mother instructing a dutiful son. It's a beautiful intimation of a vile sinner restored through grace with a compassionate wife enabling the journey.

After the devastation of the death of her first son, we read that David comforted his wife and she gave birth to a second son. David named the boy Solomon, meaning 'Peace.' God, however had a double reward for this child because He sent the prophet Nathan to bestow on him a second name, Jedidiah, which means 'Loved by the Lord.' Solomon was to become the wisest man who ever lived and the builder of one of the seven wonders of the world, the Temple in Jerusalem. He's the author of three books of the Tanakh[20] and two psalms.

But there is more. It seems that after this disastrous start, David lost interest in any wife except Bathsheba. Three more sons were born to them: Nathan, Shammua, and Shobab. Interestingly Jesus, the Messiah is a descendant of Nathan through Mary, while the stepfather of Jesus (Joseph) traces his line through Solomon.[21] So we see that not only is Jesus descended in His incarnation through David, but also through Bathsheba, his last wife. Twenty-eight generations and some thousand years later in the city of Bethlehem, a Saviour was born who is Christ the Lord; a Savior who proudly proclaims, *"I am the root and offspring of David; the Bright and Morning Star."* (Revelation 22:16)

There are more blessings to come. We read in Song of Solomon 3:11:

"See King Solomon with the crown with which his mother crowned him on the day of his wedding, the day of the gladness of his heart."

I cannot recall of another incident in the Bible of a mother crowning her son. Solomon held his mother in the greatest esteem. He was probably not yet twenty when he inherited the throne. He had two wise advisers: his mum and Nathan. He commissioned a throne for Bathsheba, and she sat at his right hand. It's my belief that as long as Bathsheba lived, Solomon was a wise and godly king. It was probably after his mother's death that his heart turned away.[22]

The Bible tells us that all things work together for good to them that love God, who are called for His purpose. All things? Even bad things? Yes, if we handle them wisely. Someone has said, "Make your sorrows work for you." This is exactly what Bathsheba did. She epitomizes the agape love we find in 1 Corinthians 13, the love that covers a multitude of sins. Or, as we find it in the New King James Version:

> "Love bears all things, believes all things, hopes all things, endures all things. Love never fails. Love never gives up."

> "Love cares more for others than for self. Love doesn't fly off the handle, doesn't keep a score of the sins of others." (The Message)

When we pray as Jesus taught us, we say, *"Forgive us our sins, as we forgive those who sin against us."* If we fail to forgive even the most heinous crimes, we will not make it into God's kingdom, for no unforgiveness can enter therein. Bathsheba is a shining example of the power and rewards of forgiveness — she was a forgiving bride.

7
Esther, The Valiant Bride

We read that Esther was beautiful in form and in face. It was her very beauty that put her in danger. When a childish and despotic Emperor lost his temper with his wife, his nobles suggested that a search be made for beautiful young virgins to be found for him to replace the disgraced Queen. It was an extensive search, for King Ahasuerus ruled over 127 Persian dominions.[23] The unfortunate young women were taken, banged up in a harem and beautified for an entire year before being escorted to the King's bed to await his pleasure. If they did not please him, they were sent back to a lifetime of seclusion in a second harem.

Personally, (forgive me!) though much has been romanticized about 'One Night with the King', I find this narrative sordid and abusive. My sympathies lie entirely with young Esther. My heart goes out to her, for she was an orphan, having lost both parents at a young age. It seems that her nearest relative was a cousin, the devout Jewish lawyer, Mordecai. Esther's real name was Hadassah, meaning Myrtle. This name connotes youth, virginity, and innocence. Evidently, it was not politically astute to be known as a Jew, so Mordecai had probably renamed her Esther, significantly meaning, Star.

So we find Esther wrested from her loving Jewish environment into the confines of the King's harem. Here we discover that this young lady is not only outwardly beautiful, but she shines everywhere with an inner radiance. There is a refrain that runs through her story: *"She obtained favour...*" It seems that everyone who came in contact with her loved her, for she was perfumed with purity. What a testimony! Away from all that is familiar, we find her now in the Persian palace surrounded by eunuchs and Persian maids. Yet, here she shines as a star illuminating her environment. She is probably fifteen or sixteen. Let us hear what people thought about her:

> "The young woman pleased him, and she obtained his favour." (Esther 2:9) That is the voice Hegai, the eunuch in charge of the virgins.

> Esther 2:15 says, "Esther obtained favour in the sight of **all who saw her."**

> And finally, after her night with the King we read,

> "The King loved Esther more than all the other women, and she obtained grace and favour in his sight more than **all** the other virgins; so he set a royal upon her head and made her Queen instead of Vashi."

If this were a conventional love story, we might read, "And they lived happily ever after." Not quite. Esther is sent back to her own royal quarters to be guarded by several eunuchs and attended by seven Persian maids. Now she is separated from the one man who truly loves her, Mordecai. Thankfully his love and care for Hadassah never fails. Every day he patrols the palace grounds and enquires after her welfare. Mordecai is a type of the Holy Spirit who always jealously guards the bride of Christ.

Enter the Evil Enemy in the guise of Haman the Agagite. His mandate is to *"steal, kill and destroy."* He has risen to power as the King's advisor and confidante. He has a plan to annihilate every Jew in all of the hundred and twenty-seven Persian provinces. He will put them to death and plunder their goods. Does this sound familiar? (I am writing this on Holocaust Memorial Day.)

Haman's plan sounds like a good idea to the King. He takes off his signet ring and hands it to Haman. The ring is very powerful. Once a decree is written, the scroll is rolled and sealed with the imprint of the King's ring. That edict cannot be broken or overturned. The death sentence is now set in concrete: every Jew must be exterminated.

Hearing of this, Mordecai is distraught. He tears his clothes and puts on sackcloth. He covers his head with ashes. He sends a message to the queen, *"Who knows but you have come to the kingdom for such a time as this?"* Esther must go to the King, reveal her true identity, and plead with him for her own life and the life of every Jew.

At the time of the decree, Esther has been Queen for four long years. She is a trophy wife and hardly sees the King. She has no voice. Worse still, to have the temerity to come into his presence without an invite may lead to death. *"He has but one law to put all to death."* If the king is in a good mood and someone barges in uninvited, he might just hold out his golden scepter and allow the supplicant to live.

Esther is now some twenty years old, and her dilemma is great. Firstly, to go to the King may mean certain death. On the other hand, if she does not go, she and all her people will certainly be killed. Not only does she need to go uninvited to the King, but she also needs to reveal her true identity. She has been masquerading as a Persian, but in reality, she is Jewish. She makes the momentous decision to put her life on the line.[24]

Esther's Plan of Action

I find this so exciting. Esther is so obviously a lady who knows her God. *"The people that know their God shall be strong and carry out great exploits."* (Daniel 11:32)

I love her plan of action:

1. **She laid her life on the line.** *"I will go to the King, which is against the law, and if I perish, I perish."* (Esther 4:16)

2. **She would not take such a risk without prayer backing.**

3. **The prayer was to be intensified by extreme fasting.** This was to be a corporate fast: Esther, her maidservants, and the entire Jewish diaspora would spend three days and three nights in the presence of the Lord. They would neither eat nor drink but cry out to the Most High for a stay of execution.

A corporate complete fast is extremely powerful. After three days of waiting before the Lord, Esther rises up and reclaims her identity as Queen. She dons her royal robes and her crown and stands before the most powerful man alive. In great weakness and trembling, she awaits his response. Will she be allowed access or be put to death?

There is something so winsome about weakness. In fact, weakness is a winner! God uses the weak things of this world to confound the strong. I like to believe that her courage and vulnerability awakened a latent feeling in the heart of Ahasuerus; a feeling called love! Seated on his magnificent throne, he extends the golden scepter and invites her into his presence. He offers the 'magic' words,

> What do you wish Queen Esther? What is your request? **It shall be given to you even to half the kingdom!** (Esther 5:6)

What an astounding answer to pray! Here we see the power of agonizing prayer and a corporate complete fast. But there is more to come…

I love and admire the wisdom of this young queen. In response to the King's magnanimous offer, she simply says, I would love you to come to dinner with me![25] Someone wisely said, "The way to a man's heart is through his stomach!"

Now the king is intrigued; whatever is his young wife up to? So that evening, Esther comes before the King. A second time he extends to her his scepter. Again he promises to give her **anything she asks.** Esther, guided by the Holy Spirit, simply asks him to come to another banquet, but this time they should be joined by his favorite minister, Haman. What neither the King nor Esther knew is that very day Haman has erected gallows on which to hang Mordecai.

That night, the King could not sleep so he asks for the records of his reign to be read to him. He learns that some time ago Mordecai foiled an assassination plot against him.

First thing that morning he orders Haman to publicly honor the Jew he hates more than anyone else—Mordecai.

Now we come to the denouement; for me the most exciting chapter of the book. The scene is the second banquet with King Ahasuerus and Haman as the honoured guests. Esther serves the King with his favorite delicacies and plies him with the choicest wine. He is like putty in her hands! A third time he holds out the golden scepter—**what on earth does she want?** At last here it is:

> "If I have found favour in your sight, O king, and if it pleases the King, let my life be given me at my petition and my people at my request. For we have been sold, my people and I, to be destroyed, to be killed and to be annihilated." (Esther 7:3, 4)

The king is shocked and outraged. Who would want to kill his winsome wife? Hadassah speaks, *"An adversary and an enemy, this wicked Haman!"* And that is it—the 'coup de maître,'—the master stroke! It's all over for the Evil Enemy. He is hanged on the gallows he had prepared for Mordecai. Mordecai becomes the Prime Minister with the ring of authority to make laws, statutes, and decrees.

The book closes with a picture of the Holy Spirit and the Bride ruling and reigning together, passing just laws and decrees. The entire Jewish race has been saved from destruction, the King is now in love with his wife, and there is peace in the land.

> "Mordecai the Jew was second in command to King Ahasuerus and was great among the Jews… seeking the good of his people and speaking peace to all his countrymen." (Esther 10:3)

PART THREE
The Bride Price

8
The Cost to the Father

The Bible is the most exciting love story ever, and every one of its 66 books can tell us something of the passionate love of God the Father for us, His children, and the passionate love of the Lord Jesus Christ for us, His bride. The story of Abraham and Isaac in Genesis 22 is a powerful illustration of the agonizing cost of our salvation. Verse one begins ominously, *"After these things God **tested** Abraham."* What things?

In Genesis 15, God promises Abram that his descendants will be more than the stars in the heavens. (Google tells me there are one hundred thousand million of them.) Almighty God and Abram then cut a covenant. This means everything that God has He will give to Abram and potentially, everything Abram owns he may give to God. The two parties also promise to protect each other.

So, in Chapter 22 when God calls Abraham, He is about to put His covenant partner to the test. He calls him and immediately Abraham responds, **"Hineni!"** I love this Hebrew word. It's a military word. It means, "Here I am." Implying "I'm here, standing at attention ready to receive and obey your orders." The orders are extremely shocking.

> "Take your son, your **only son,** Isaac, **whom you love** and go to the land of Moriah and offer him there as a burnt offering."

A burnt offering was when the entire animal was slaughtered then burnt on the altar as a sweet aroma to the

THE ULTIMATE WEDDING

Lord. Abraham has waited twenty-five long years for Isaac—Laughter—the son of promise, the one from whom will come millions of descendants.

But doesn't God forbid child sacrifice? Which loving father would bind, kill, and burn his only son? And yet... (this is mind blowing) Abraham so trusts God as his Covenant Partner that he does not hesitate. The very next morning early Abraham, Isaac, a servant, and a donkey take the wood, the fire, and the knife and set off on a 3-day journey to Mt. Moriah, Jerusalem (the site of Calvary). Imagine the pain in Abraham's heart on that long journey. As far as Isaac knew, he and his father were there to worship the living God. It was only when they reached Mt Moriah that Isaac was told there was no animal. He was to be the sacrifice.

Opinions vary as to the age of Isaac, ranging from seventeen to thirty. Amazingly, Isaac so trusts and loves his father that he prepares to die. He is young, strong, and fit. He could have overpowered his father and run back to mum. Isaac willingly offered himself up to the altar and the knife. We now know it was not necessary. It was a test. Isaac did not know that. Isaac allowed himself to be bound to the altar as a living sacrifice to be killed by his own father. Here we have a picture of the perfect Son put to death by His own Father; the innocent Lamb of God slain for sinners.

Shortly after the binding, Isaac was rewarded with a bride. His father sent his servant on a five-hundred-mile journey to search for a bride from his own extended family. Isaac was passive; the bride price had been paid. Abraham is a type of God the Father. Isaac shows us God the Son. The servant is a type of the Holy Spirit. Almighty God sent His Holy Spirit to find you so that you could become the bride of Christ.

The Cost to the Father

2,400 years later there was no stay of execution. The Lord Jesus Christ dwelt in an atmosphere so pure, so holy that we can hardly imagine it. Together with the Father and the Holy Spirit, Jesus was worshipped by angels and archangels. He was robed in splendor and crowned with glory.

When the Father said, *"Whom shall I send and who will go for Me?"* Our Lord responded, *"Hineni!" Here am I! Send Me."* Jesus was the God-man born to die. For three years He set His face like a flint towards Calvary. He was not bound to an altar, but to a cross. No Angel. No voice from heaven. No ram in a thicket. No reprieve.

> Hebrews 5:7 says, "In the days of His flesh (Jesus) when He has offered up prayers and supplications with **vehement cries and tears** to Him who was able to save Him from death and was heard because of His godly fear."

Yes, He was heard, **but there was no reprieve.** The Father told His Son, "There is no other way. You have to become sin and You have to do this **alone.** I can't look on sin. The Holy Spirit can't help You. It's You and Satan face to face." ***"Though He was a Son, yet He learned obedience by the things which He suffered."*** (Hebrews 5:8) Only when we reach God's Presence will we fully understand the depth of Christ's suffering on the cross. He did it for you. He did it for me.

> "Jesus, the author and finisher of our faith... for the joy that was set before Him endured the cross, despising the shame, and has sat down at the right hand of the throne of God." (Hebrews 12:2)

What joy made Him endure? It was our redemption from the slavery of sin and Satan. HALLELUJAH! Selah! Pause and think about it...

Imagine you are on that three-day trek to the site of Calvary. You are Abram. Think about the anguish, the turmoil in your heart. You are covenanted to Almighty God. Under the terms of the covenant, He can ask *anything* of you. What is dearest to your heart? Would you be able to surrender it to your Father? Abram had a reprieve and a reward. For God our Father and His only begotten Son, there was to be no other way.

We know Jesus agonized in the garden. How do you think His Father suffered? What did it cost Him to pour out His wrath on the Son of His love? We know that God is angry with the sinner every day. That is you and me. Our Holy God hates sin. It cannot enter His Presence. I simply cannot grasp the depth of the anguish of the Father in heaven as His Son was nailed to the cross. As Jesus was *being made sin,* all the Father could do was to cover the crucifixion sight with thick darkness so that no one could witness the utter degradation, the shocking ugliness of the Son as He took upon Himself billions of sins of billions of people.

God could not watch. The Holy Spirit withdrew, leaving our Saviour to bear the cost totally and utterly alone. What did it cost the Holy Spirit stand by and do nothing? This is the stupendous price of our redemption from the power of sin and Satan.

9
The Cost to the Son

It was in the Garden of Gethsemane that the real agony began. From eternity, our Lord Jesus had known that He was to be the sacrificial Lamb Who *"takes away the sin of the world."*[26] Gethsemane means olive press. The olives were placed between two huge millstones and squeezed until every drop of oil was extracted. In that garden, surrounded by olive trees and sleeping disciples, Jesus was pressed beyond measure. He was in mental and emotional agony as He faced the ordeal ahead. Not only that, but He was also greatly afraid. In fact, He was so fearful that He sweat great drops of blood. Imagine! Why was He afraid? Let us not forget that though He was fully God, He was also fully man. He was about to be MADE SIN. He was to take on your sin, my sin, and the sins of billions of others.

> "For He who knew no sin became SIN for us, that we might become the righteousness of God in Him." (2 Corinthians 5:21)

The weight of our sin was so fearful that it nearly killed Him. If that was not enough, something else was weighing Him down, pressing Him almost beyond endurance. For the first time ever, Father and Son were to be separated. Our thrice-Holy God cannot look on sin. He hates sin. He is angry with the wicked every day. His great wrath was about to be poured out on the sin of mankind and that angry wrath would land on His Only Begotten Son as He hung helpless on the cross. Perhaps we should pause here to remember with gratitude the total agony of the Father and the Holy Spirit as they turned away from the sin-besieged Son. We can imagine the holy silence in heaven. Little wonder that the Father had to send angels to strengthen Jesus in that garden of desperation. How poignant that His only friends in the garden were the angels.

Now strengthened for the torture ahead, He arose to meet His accusers. It was probably around nine o'clock that evening. Throughout the night He was pushed from pillar to post, enduring scoffing, ribaldry, the painful betrayal by Peter, and three mock trials. By 8 am Friday morning, He was before Pilate, accused of high treason. Pilate could find no fault in Him but capitulated to the mob.

Jesus had already been publicly humiliated. His beard had been pulled out. He was hit on the head, slapped on the face, spat upon, dressed as a king and mocked. His crown was made of thorns some nine inches long, rammed onto His head causing the blood to flow down His face. Now he was stripped naked to be scourged. He was bound to a post and a leather whip with many thongs loaded with lead, spikes, and bones, was lashed upon His back thirty-nine times. All the flesh was torn from His back. This was the 'intermediate death.'

As He shouldered the cross to ascend to Golgotha, He was already dying. Loss of blood and the weight of the cross caused Him to collapse. He had neither eaten nor drunk since the last supper with the disciples. On that upward climb, He thought of YOU. He thought of me. What was that joy? **He was paying the price for His bride.**

"For we have not been redeemed with corruptible things like silver or gold, but with the precious blood of Jesus as of a lamb without blemish and without spot." (1 Peter 1:18, 19)

"He was led as a lamb to the slaughter, and as a sheep before its shearers is silent, so He opened not His mouth." (Isaiah 53:7)

At noon our Lord was nailed to the cross, and just three hours later, at three in the afternoon—the time of the evening sacrifice—He was dead. In the Temple below the cross, thousands of Passover lambs were being ritually slaughtered.

Three Dreadful Hours That Changed The World

From twelve noon to 3 pm, thick darkness covered Jerusalem. These were the three most distressing hours any individual has ever endured. It was then the Father left, abandoning His Son to His fate. The Holy Spirit withdrew. There was deep silence in heaven. The angels watched in horror. For those three hours, Jesus was **made sin.** God the Father cannot look on sin. He is the thrice-Holy God *"dwelling in unapproachable light."* (1 Timothy 6:16) Not only was the earth darkened, but Jesus Himself entered into darkness: body, soul, and spirit. He cries out in anguish, *"My God, My God, why have You forsaken me?"* (Matthew 27:46)

As the devil and all his demons danced round, Jesus became the ultimate atonement: our Kinsman Redeemer. Sin is not a pretty sight; it is vile, abominable and it stinks. *"I am a worm and no man; a reproach of men and despised by the people. All who see Me ridicule Me."* (Psalm 22: 6, 7) Isaiah puts it this way: *"He has no stately form or splendor and no beauty that we should desire Him."* The most beautiful Man ever became gruesomely ugly and contorted by sin.

I find it hard to describe how disgusting He became. All I know is that the sight was so ghastly that God had to cover Him, who was covered in sin, with thick darkness as He hung alone suspended between heaven and hell. He died of a ruptured, broken heart. Can we say that sin killed Him, our sin? The songwriter says, *"He died my death; He paid my price that I may live."*

The Centurion marveled that He could die so quickly. Just to make sure, one of the soldiers took his lance and plunged it into his victim's side; the lining of Christ's heart releasing a flow of blood and water.

> "Without shedding of blood there is no remission [forgiveness of sin]." (Hebrews 9:22)

And that is how the Bride, the church of God, was born. As Eve was 'born' from Adam so we, the church, were 'born' from the wounded heart of Christ.

> "Unless one is born of water and the Spirit, he cannot enter the Kingdom of God." (John 3:5)

Some four thousand years before the crucifixion the Lord God caused His Adam, (Ish) to fall into a deep, painless sleep. From the side of His sleeping son, He took a rib and fashioned it into 'Ishah', a woman; a helper suitable and commensurate with him; a bride whom he could love and cherish, a bride who would bring him joy. Together they would rule, reign, and have dominion. Together they would be fruitful and multiply.

And so, from the tortured body of the Second Adam was born a beautiful helper commensurate with her Lord—an earthly bride for a heavenly Bridegroom. The bride is you. The bride is me; the ekklesia, the called-out ones.

The price: the greatest mental, emotional, physical, and spiritual torment that has ever been known. What a Savior!

> "Greater love has no one than this, than to lay down one's life for his friends." (John 15:13)

What father on earth would want his son to suffer such ignominy, such torture? Yet this the agony of our Father in heaven, holding back, restraining the angels, pouring the wrath we deserve on His only beloved Son. Let us worship and adore our Father for such a supreme sacrifice.

10
The Seven Wounds of Jesus
And How They Set Us Free

In the wonderful song, *Here I Am To Worship*, Chris Tomlin writes, *"I'll never know how much it cost to see my sin upon that cross."* Will we ever be able to grasp the cost Jesus paid for our salvation? We will never know the full extent this side of heaven, but we can certainly try, perhaps by looking at the wounds He bore for us:

Blood is a very precious commodity. We cannot live without it. *"The life is in the blood"* and *"According to the law, almost all things are purified with blood, and without shedding of blood there is no remission."* (Leviticus 17:11, Hebrews 9:22) Sins remitted! Sins forgiven! What a glorious reality. Let us look again at the cost: the last terrifying eighteen hours of the life of our Lord and Savior, examining what His wounds mean to us today.

1. SWEATING BLOOD IN THE GARDEN:
Mental Anguish

"In the days of His flesh, (Jesus) offered up prayers and supplications with vehement cries and tears to Him who was able to save Him from death, and was heard because of His godly fear (reverent submission). Though He was a Son, yet He learned obedience by the things which He suffered." (Hebrews 5:7, 8)

Yes, He was heard: *"Let this suffering pass from Me."* (Matthew 26:39) But the answer was, "No. You have to go through the fire. There is no other payment for sin but Your blood."

Have you ever suffered intense pain and extreme mental anguish? Jesus is your High Priest who has been in all points tempted like you and me. Jesus sweat blood. This is a recognized medical condition called hematidrosis. It is caused when the capillary blood vessels feeding the sweat glands rupture. It occurs under conditions of extreme emotional or physical stress. Some of the soldiers in the trenches in World War 2 sweat blood before they were gunned down. Have you ever suffered that type of stress? As angels strengthened Jesus for His ordeal, the Holy Spirit (your Comforter) will strengthen you. *"Surely He has borne our griefs and carried our sorrows."* (Isaiah 53:4)

2. HIS CROWN OF THORNS:
Rejection and Sorrow

"The soldiers of the Governor took Jesus into the Praetorium and gathered the whole garrison around Him (600 men), and they stripped him and put a scarlet robe on Him. When they had twisted a crown of thorns, they put it on His head and a reed in His right hand. And they bowed the knee before Him, and mocked Him, saying, 'Hail, King of the Jews.' Then they spat upon Him." (Matthew 27:27-30)

The thorns were cruel, not just physically, but emotionally. "You say you are a King. Here's your crown." It was not gold, encrusted with jewels, but sharp thorns some nine inches long rammed into our Lord's head, causing profuse bleeding. Wonderfully, it sets us free from rejection, cursing, devaluation, and every unkind word or curse spoken over us!

3. HIS BRUISING & INTERNAL BLEEDING: Iniquities and Peace

Firstly, by the Jews:

> "Now the men who held Jesus mocked Him and beat Him. And having blindfolded Him, they struck Him on the face and asked Him saying, 'Prophesy! Who is the one who struck you?' And many other things they blasphemously spoke against Him." (Luke 22:63)

And by the Romans:

> "Then they spat on Him and took the reed and struck Him on the head." (Matthew 27:30)

Let us remember these second beatings were from 600 hardened soldiers. This aggressive and violent assault caused deep, internal bruising. *He was bruised for our iniquities; the chastisement for our peace was upon Him.* (Isaiah 53:5) Have you ever suffered extreme stress, sleepless nights, or beatings? There is healing for you in the cross of Jesus Christ.

4. HIS SCOURGING:
Healing for Every Sickness

Matthew simply says," *When they had scourged Him, (Pilate)* delivered *Him to be crucified.*" (27:26) Do not be misled. This flogging was so severe it was known as the intermediate death. In fact, some criminals actually died under these lashes. The scourge was a whip with many leather strands. Each leather throng had glass, nails, and sharp bones embedded in it. As the whip struck the victim's back, it was dragged down, ripping off the skin, tearing through muscles and nerves. Imagine that thirty-nine times! The Psalmist prophesied, "*The plowers plowed on my back: they made their furrows long.*" (Psalm 129:3) When the soldiers had finished, the back of our beautiful Savior was like a mass of raw meat, so much so He did not even look human:

"His appearance was so disfigured beyond that of any human being and his form marred beyond human likeness." (Isaiah 52:14 NIV)

Oh holy and obedient Lord! "*And by His stripes we are healed.*" (Isaiah 53:5) Physicians tell us there are thirty-nine major illnesses. The stripes of Jesus heal every single one. The blood of Jesus heals you.

5. HIS NAILED HANDS:
Freedom from Beatings and Cruelty

(Pilate) *"delivered Him to be crucified."* (John 19:16) Crucifixion is the cruelest form of death. It was reserved for criminals and non-Romans. The iron nails that hammered the hands and feet of Jesus were four sided, and fifteen centimeters long; forcefully driven in by a leaden mallet. They caused total agony! These are the hands that blessed little children, washed the disciple's feet, healed lepers, and raised the dead. We too can use our hands to heal, to bless, and to serve.

6. HIS NAIL PIERCED FEET:
Deliverance from our Past

The blood that oozed down the cross from the feet of Jesus reminds us that if our feet have taken us to places of shame, our past can be totally forgiven. Our feet can be redeemed!

> "How beautiful on the mountains are the feet of him who brings good news, who proclaims peace, who brings glad tidings of good things, who proclaims salvation, who says to Zion, 'Your God Reigns!'" (Isaiah 52:7)

7. HIS PIERCED SIDE:
Sin paid for, Satan defeated, & the birth of the Bride

Here we have the most poignant wound. Only the Apostle John reveals this last assault on the dead body of our Lord.

> "One of the soldiers pierced His side with a spear, and immediately blood and water came out." (John 19:34)

From this wounded side of Jesus, the Bride of Christ was born. Jesus is the second Adam. Just as Eve came forth from the side of Adam, so we—His bride—were born of water and of blood. This is no ordinary blood. It is the blood of the spotless Lamb of God who was slain before the foundation of the world. Oh, the precious, priceless blood! It is the most valuable commodity this world has ever known. *"Without the shedding of blood there is no remission"* [of sin]. (Hebrews 9:22)

Later John comments on this wound in his first letter:

"This is He who came by water and blood—Jesus Christ; not only by water, but by water and blood." (1 John 5:6)

There is a fountain filled with blood
drawn from Immanuel's veins
And sinners plunged beneath that flood
Lose all their guilty stains.

Halleluiah! What a Saviour! Jesus Christ by His shed blood... *"is able to save to the uttermost those who come to God through Him, since He always lives to make intercession for them."* (Hebrews 7:25)

This not the blood of bulls or goats, but the ultimate sacrifice; the sacrifice to end all sacrifices.

Where is the Blood Today?

The book of Hebrews states that Jesus' blood is before the throne of God in the heavenly Holy of Holies.

"For Christ has not entered the holy places made with hands which are copies of the true, but into heaven itself, now to appear in the presence of God for us; not to offer Himself often…. but now, at the end of the ages, He has appeared **to put away sin** by the sacrifice of Himself." (Hebrews 9:24-26)

I like to think about the world-shaking event when Jesus spectacularly entered heaven to the standing ovation of angels, archangels, cherubim, and seraphim! He bowed before His Father with eight pints of His pure and precious blood while heaven rang with applause, adulation, and joy! God, the Father looks upon that blood and says to us, *"When I see the blood, I will pass over you."* (Exodus 12:13)

Jesus triumphantly bearing His own blood delivers us *"from the fear of death, we who all our lifetime were subject to bondage."* (Hebrews 2:15) And together with all the hosts of heaven, *"We see Jesus… for the suffering of death crowned with glory and honour, that He by the grace of God, might taste death for everyone."* (Hebrews 2:9)

So to recap, the precious blood of Jesus:

- Cleanses us from sin and allows us to be 'born again' into the family of God.
- It heals us from mental anguish.
- It sets us free from rejection and sorrow.
- It binds our iniquities to the cross and gives us peace.
- Heals all our diseases.
- Heals us from cruelty inflicted by others, and
- Delivers us from our past bad memories and sins.

The heroic sacrifice on the cross sets us wonderfully free from every bondage. The Bride Price was paid. We were ransomed from slavery to Satan. All sin is paid for, and our nakedness was covered. Every sickness is dealt with, and every curse is broken. Every heartache, rejection, reproach, and shame taken away. All mental anguish is removed, and all emotional trauma is healed. This is the total freedom Jesus has won for each one of us.

"If the Son shall set you free, you shall be free indeed." (John 8:36)

PART FOUR
Our Heavenly Bridegroom

11

Beholding Our King

"Your eyes shall see the King in His beauty."
(Isaiah 33:17)

How do you picture Jesus? As a cute baby, a carpenter, or perhaps a crucified corpse? So many artists present Him in these ways: a sweet and helpless baby with BIG mama; a wimpy looking itinerant preacher with fair hair, or the corpse on the cross as dead as can be. If that is your impression of Jesus, please forget it. So many artists have missed the fact that Jesus was and is Jewish. He is 'Yeshua HaMashiach', The Messiah, The Anointed One. As a carpenter, he was strong and muscular, an alpha male. It has been estimated that on a typical day Jesus walked twenty miles. In his lifetime, He walked a staggering 21,500 miles; almost enough to encircle the globe. Those were the days when willingly our Lord laid aside His majesty and His Kingly splendour.

But now — with the eyes of faith — we can begin to glimpse Him as He truly is. The Ultimate Hero of the Universe is simply indescribable. Writing these last chapters, I can only ask the help of the Holy Spirit, and whatever I write will be a pale reflection of who He really is. But let's try:

The carpenter is now a King, actually not a king, but THE KING, King of Kings and Lord of Lords. John the Baptist saw Him as *"the Lamb of God that takes away the sin of the world."* But the crucified Lamb is now a risen Lion with a roar that fills the stratosphere. While on earth, Christ declared that He was the Light of the world, but now He is **The** Light of Heaven. The Shekinah glory of our Lord shines brighter than a million suns. We know that our sun is a raging ball of fire with a temperature of 14 million degrees Celsius. Then consider this: the raging ball of fire that is our sun is merely a candle in comparison to the radiance of our Lord. Little wonder that our redeemed bodies will need redeemed retinas!

The glory of the Risen Lord is so stupendous that the few people who have been privileged to glimpse Him have fallen at His feet like dead men:

- Paul was blinded for three days and knocked to the ground. (Acts 9:3)
- John, the beloved, *"fell at His feet as dead."* (Revelation 1:17)
- Ezekiel fell on his face. (Ezekiel 1:28, 3:23)
- Daniel encountering the Angel Gabriel and *"fainted and was sick for days."* (Daniel 8:27)
- When we come face to face with the Holy One, we can only cry out with Isaiah,

"Woe is me, for I am undone! Because I am a man of unclean lips, and I dwell in the midst of a people of unclean lips; for my eyes have seen the King, the Lord of hosts." (Isaiah 6:5)

Through seeing Him, we see ourselves. We see that our supposed righteousness is as filthy rags in His sight.[27] We cry out with Job,

"I have heard of You by the hearing of the ear, but now my eye sees You. Therefore I abhor myself and repent in dust and ashes." (Job 42:5, 6)

So let us endeavor to discover Jesus as He is now — highly exalted with a Name above every other name. He's the Light of heaven, the Hero above all heroes, forever worshipped, forever glorified, forever glorious.

And yet, this is The One, The Holy One, the Ultimate Bridegroom who has chosen us to be His Bride. How shall we describe this Indescribable One? His Infallible Word describes Him as: **Our Mighty Warrior** and **The Greatest Hero of all Time.**

OUR MIGHTY WARRIOR

I once had a vision. I saw a huge subterranean prison populated by seemingly endless prison cells stretching as far as the eye could see. The atmosphere was dank and fetid, encased in a pervasive gloom. Each cell housed a solitary prisoner chained by the neck and ankles. Unspeakable shrieks and moans filled the air. The stench was overpowering. Outside each prison cell was a long list of each prisoners' crimes.[28] The corridors were patrolled by thousands of gleeful demons.

As I watched and listened, suddenly there was an earthquake and then lightning; a bolt so bright that the entire prison was filled with light. Then I saw that it was not lightning at all. It was the Risen Lord in all His radiant glory. As He stood magnificent in splendor surveying the scene, the demons fell backwards paralysed by fear. The Head Jailor, still standing, became a quivering mass. The

Risen Lord strode towards him and with a voice that thundered, cried out, "I'll have these!" He snatched the keys of Death and Hell and triumphantly held them aloft.[29] The earthquake had opened every cell door, but as Jesus took the keys of death and hell, every chain fell off and every prisoner was freed.

There was one more thing to do. As I watched, I saw the Lord Jesus Christ on a rampage. Running to every cell door, He violently removed every list of sins, tearing them up into hundreds of pieces.

This is our Warrior King: God's El Gibor, the Avenger, the One we worship. On that hideous cross, our Lord comprehensively, utterly, finally, once and for all defeated Satan, the Evil Enemy. In that ghastly prison where you and I deserve to be, He took your key, opened the door, loosed your chains, and set you free. He tore up the lists of our crimes and nailed a new decree to every prison door—FREE PARDON. The wonder is He did all this single-handedly. This great Warrior is the Avenger of Blood. He is the One spoken of in Isaiah 61: 1-6:

> "The Spirit of the Lord God is upon Me because the Lord has anointed Me to preach good tidings to the poor. He has sent Me to heal the brokenhearted, to proclaim liberty to the captives, and the opening of the prison to those that are bound; to proclaim the acceptable year of the Lord, and the day of vengeance of our God; to comfort all who mourn, to console those who mourn in Zion, to give them beauty for ashes, the oil of joy for mourning, the garment of praise for the spirit of heaviness." (Luke 4:18-19)

Here we see Jesus, the Warrior filled with burning rage against God's enemies. This is Jesus, the Serpent Slayer, the One who *"treads the winepress alone,"* trampling them in anger, trampling in fury, with blood-stained garments. This is The One whose *"own fury sustained"* Him as there was none to help:

"I looked but there was no one to help, I wondered that there was no one to uphold; therefore My own arm brought salvation for Me." (Isaiah 63:5)

Single-handedly our Saviour defeated Satan. Great David's greater Son slew a giant a million times more powerful than Goliath and paradoxically He did it by becoming a lamb.

Jesus, the Messiah and our Lord is our El Gibor. This is one of my favourite names for the Lord Jesus Christ. El is God, El Gibor is the Mighty God, the Hero, the Champion. The Hebrew root is geber, meaning Man of Valour, and man at the height of his manly power. Even before He returns for us, at this moment and forever, He is our Redeemer, our Mighty Warrior who has comprehensively set us free from the dominion of Satan and his Evil Empire.

We can liken Him to St. George, the patron saint of England, who famously, according to legend, slew the dragon. He is often portrayed as a glorious figure, blood-stained sword victoriously aloft, and his foot firmly on the neck of a fearsome dragon. Every hero of every book is but a pale reflection of the Hero of all heroes who single-handedly dealt with sin and Satan, rescuing His bride from certain and eternal death and damnation.

THE GREATEST HERO OF ALL TIME

The Bible is replete with mysteries and here we have perhaps the greatest mystery that a thrice Holy God who dwells in light unapproachable and is a Consuming Fire should make the huge descent from Pure Light to gross darkness to seek and to save lost mankind.

> "For God SO LOVED the world that He sent His Only Begotten Son, that whosoever believes in Him should not perish, but have everlasting life. For God did not send His Son into the world to condemn the world, but that the world through Him might be saved." (John 3:16, 17)

Here we have 007, the greatest hero of all time. Imagine the scene in heaven as the Creator of the Universe, the Express Image of The Father, the Only One to be begotten (not created) divested Himself of every glory and left the wonder of the heavenly realm to descend, descend, descend. Leaving the third heaven, He passes through the realm of the prince of this world, enters the sin-filled atmosphere of planet Earth and arrives in Nazareth. Here, surrendering to the Holy Spirit, watched over by the archangel Gabriel, He is imprinted into the womb of a young girl. What grace! Such vulnerability! He is now entirely dependent on his teenage mother.

> *How silently, how silently the wondrous gift is given. So God imparts to human hearts the wonders of His heaven.*[30]

Silently, secretly the Christ child enters the world He created. He survives a murderous attempt by King Herod as His 'parents' rush him to Egypt by night. Only after the King's demise, do they return undercover to Nazareth. For the next thirty years He lives a seemingly unremarkable life as a craftsman under the tutelage of his stepfather. Image a child who never had a tantrum, a teenager who never stalked out slamming the door behind Him, a young adult unfailingly kind and courteous; the perfect Man. It is not that He was never tempted to sin. The glory is that He was "in all points tempted as we are, yet without sin." If He had ever "lost it" just once, we would be lost forever. Selah!

One day, he left his tools, his mother, and his home and walked down to the Jordan River. There the sinless Son of God submitted to the waters of baptism. As he came up out of the water, the heavens were opened, the Holy Spirit descended upon Him, and the voice of His Father proclaimed, *"You are My beloved Son, in whom I am well pleased."* So begins the three-year journey to the cross and lower still to the depths of hell.

The Apostle Paul puts it this way:

> "Although being essentially one with God and in the form of God (possessing the fullness ad attributes which make God God), did not think this equality with God was a thing to be eagerly grasped or retained; stripped Himself (of all privileges and rightful dignity) assumed the guise of a slave and became a human being. After He had appeared in human form He abased and humbled Himself, carrying His obedience to the extreme of death, even death on the cross." (Philippians 2:6–8 Amplified)

So a man, a bondslave, a crucified corpse! His descent continued into the very pit of hell, where He *"disarmed principalities and powers and made a public spectacle of them, triumphing over them (by the cross.)"* (Colossians 2:15) The King of all glory disguised as a common criminal wrought the greatest victory of all time defeating sin, disarming Satan, and setting us prisoners free.

> "We see Jesus, who was made a little lower than the angels, for the suffering of death, crowned with glory and honour, that He, by the grace of God might taste death for everyone." (Hebrews 2:9)

> "Therefore God has highly exalted Him and given Him the Name which is above every other name, that at the name of Jesus every knee should bow, of those in heaven, and of those on earth, and of those under the earth, and that every tongue should confess that Jesus Christ is Lord, to the glory of God the Father." (Philippians 2:9-11)

Oh, let's give it up for Jesus the world's greatest Hero; your hero and mine. Why did He put Himself through all that? for you, for me.

> "For the joy that was set before Him, He endured the cross, despising the shame, and has sat down at the right hand of the throne of God." (Hebrews 12:2)

With His dying breath Jesus thought about us, His bride. Indeed, we have not been redeemed with corruptible things like silver or gold, but we have been purchased in the slave market, paid for in blood. Jesus looks at you and thinks it's a price worth paying.

12

The Glories of the Messiah and His Bride

Psalm 45 is a very unique messianic Psalm, entitled, *The Glories of the Messiah and His Bride*. Let's read some of its verses from the Passion Translation:

"Beautiful! Beautiful! Beyond the sons of men! Elegant grace pours out through every word You speak. Truly God has anointed You, His favored One, for eternity! Now strap Your lightning sword of judgment on Your side, O Mighty Warrior, so majestic! You are full of beauty and splendor as You go out to war! In Your glory and Your grandeur go forth to victory! Through your faithfulness and meekness, the cause of truth will stand. Awe-inspiring miracles are accomplished by Your power, leaving everyone dazed and astonished… Your Kingdom, O God, endures forever for You are enthroned to rule with a justice scepter in Your hand! You are passionate for righteousness, and You hate lawlessness. That is why God, Your God, crowns you with bliss above Your fellow kings. He has anointed You… with His oil of fervent joy, the very fragrance of heaven's gladness. Your royal robes release the scent of suffering love for Your bride; the odor of aromatic incense is upon You." (Psalm 45:1-8 TPT)

Here He is, the Lover of our souls, this Warrior King, this Bridegroom God whose glory eclipses the sun, the moon, the planets, whose face shines like a perigee sun, whose eyes blaze like fire. He is the thrice Holy God, seated at the right hand of the Father, crowned with glory and honour; worshipped by angels, archangels, and all the hosts of heaven… and He is coming for us!

This wedding psalm portrays our Heavenly Bridegroom as He is now; the Mighty Conqueror, 007, who has paid the price and executed the most daring rescue mission ever. His eyes glow with ardent love for the Bride. He tells us:

> "Behold you are fair, my love… you have ravished My heart with one look of your eyes. How fair is your love, My sister, My spouse." (Song of Solomon 1:15)

He tells us that we are…

> "As fair as the moon, clear as the sun, awesome as an army with banners." (6:10)

Not only has He defeated Satan, but He has transformed the lovers of His soul. He is ready for the Wedding. His heart throbs with passionate love; the love of a Lover for his bride. And here we are, standing at His side:

> "At Your right hand stands the queen in gold from Ophir. Listen, O daughter, Consider and incline your ear; forget your own people also, and your father's house; so the King will **greatly desire your beauty;** Because He is your Lord, worship Him… With gladness and rejoicing… they shall enter the King's Palace." (Psalm 45:9-11)

This Psalm is particularly poignant to me. Some fifty-seven years ago, four days before my wedding, my father and mother asked me to leave their house. They told me that no way could I marry from my parental home. They could not agree to my wedding. They would not attend, much less 'give me away' nor would any family member be there. My parents were not alone in their fears. Just about every 'man of God' warned me that I was making a mistake.

Brokenhearted, I left with one suitcase to the house God had given us. There I knelt before the Lord and wept my way through the Psalms. My bridegroom was some two hundred miles away in Scotland. The reason for my parent's distress — he was African and I was English. For four precious days I was alone with God. I did not fully realize this at that time, but I now know that the Lord Jesus was preparing me to be not only a bride for Paul Jinadu, but to be His very own delightful bride.

What the Holy Spirit whispered to me through my tears was life-transforming. Firstly that:

"When my father and mother forsake me, the Lord will take me up." (Psalm 27:10)

Secondly, that I am beautiful and desirable, not just to my husband to be, but to the King of Kings and Lord of Lords. This marriage was to be a pale rehearsal for the eternal union with the Creator of the Universe. Later I was to learn about agape love, the God kind of love we find in 1 Corinthians 13; the love that covers a multitude of sins. I was to discover that in laying down my life for my husband, I was, in fact, loving God whom I have not yet seen.

"If someone says, 'I love God,' and hates his brother, whom he has seen, how can he love God whom he has not seen? This commandment we have from

Him: that he who loves God must love his brother also." (1 John 4:20, 21)

Thirdly, during that time, Psalm 27 became a lodestar for my life. In my Bible it is called *"An Exuberant Declaration of Faith."* I have also called it, 'Throne Room Living.'

"The LORD is my light and my salvation: whom shall I fear? The LORD is the strength of my life; of whom shall I be afraid? Though an army encamp against me my heart shall not fear; though war rise up against me in this will I be confident. **One thing** have I desired of the Lord, that will I seek that I may dwell in the house of the Lord, all the days of my life, to behold the beauty of the Lord, and to inquire in His Temple for in the time of trouble He will hide me in His pavilion."

There, on my knees I learned with David that if I jettison the clamour, the attack and distress all around me and simply worship my Lord and Saviour, He will fight my battles and sort out my distress.

Does my story have a happy ending? Yes, indeed. Though my earthly father did not walk me to the altar, my Heavenly Father did just that. I clearly heard His voice, "I AM your Father, and I will give you away." When we returned from our honeymoon, my parents were waiting to meet us, asking for forgiveness. Four months later my husband and I sailed to Nigeria as missionaries. While we were there, my parents started attending church and surrendered their lives to Christ. Please believe me, my parents were only doing their best according to the light they had. I thank God for them and for an extremely happy and carefree childhood they gave me. They were wonderful people.

13
The Bride's Dress

When Jesus hung on the cross, He was naked. It was the ultimate degradation for the spotless Son of God. Yet, He was covered. Physically, He was covered with blood, for when He was scourged with whips, he was unclothed. But the worse was to come: our Saviour was MADE SIN. From twelve midday to three in the afternoon, thick darkness covered the land. Why? Because it was then that Jesus was made sin. He was literally covered with sin.

Sin is profoundly ugly. Sin stinks. The last three hours of our Saviour's life were so frightful that His Father chose to shroud His beloved Son with blackness. For God the Father…

> "Made Him who knew no sin to BE SIN FOR US, that we might become the righteousness of God in Him."
> (2 Corinthians 5:21)

On the cross slowly dying between two criminals your Saviour was MADE SIN. What does this mean? Think about it — your sin and mine, the sin of nine billion people was placed upon One Man, the second Adam.

> "As by one man sin entered into the world, and death through sin, thus death spread to all men because all sinned." (Romans 5:12)

The Bride's Dress

Every sin you and I have ever committed was placed on Jesus while He hung naked on the cross. He was made sin. He became an object of horror. Every rape, every murder, every unkind word, every adultery, fornication, and lust were placed on Him. The sins of nine billion people were put on our Lord. He was indeed The Scapegoat. He was the lamb without spot or blemish; the sacrifice to end all sacrifices.

"Behold! The Lamb of God who takes away the sin of the world!" (John 1:29)

"His visage (face, appearance) was marred more than any man, and His form more than the sons of men." (Isaiah 52:14)

The Passion Translation puts it this way:

"Many were appalled at the sight of Him (for so marred was His appearance, that) He NO LONGER LOOKED LIKE A MAN."

Jesus was the most beautiful, the most handsome, the most charismatic Man that has ever lived. He was full of the Holy Spirit. Everywhere He went people flocked to Him like bees to a honey pot. But on the cross…

"He had no (stately) form or comeliness (splendour). There is no beauty that we should desire Him. He is despised and rejected by men, a Man of sorrows and acquainted with grief and we hid, as it were, our faces from Him. He was despised and we did not esteem Him." (Isaiah 53:2, 3)

King David, speaking prophetically in Psalm 22, speaking as if the voice of the Lord says,

"I am a worm and no man: a reproach of men and despised by the people. I am poured out like water and all my bones are out of joint; my heart is like wax; it has melted within Me."

As He became more and more ugly, more and more disfigured, He cried out in anguish,

"My God, My God, why have You forsaken Me?"

As if in answer, the heavens opened, and the Father poured out His wrath—His anger at sin—upon the dying body of His beloved Son.

Perhaps we will never know the full price that was paid for our forgiveness this side of eternity. In the life to come it will be fully revealed, the height, the depth of the agony that Jesus experienced to set us free. Singlehandedly without the aid of His Father or of the Holy Spirit, He paid our debt and set us free forever from the clutches of the Evil One. O Hallelujah! What a Saviour!

He was naked that we might be covered.

Isaiah tells us:

"I will rejoice greatly in the Lord. My soul shall be joyful in my God, for He has clothed me with garments of salvation. He has covered me with the robe of righteousness. As a bridegroom decks himself with ornaments and as a bride adorns herself with her jewels." (Isaiah 61:10)

This is The Great Exchange. Jesus took your sin as your scapegoat. In exchange, He gave you His right standing before a Holy God. For us it is a free pardon, but for Jesus, it cost Him everything. *"Greater love has no man than this, that a man lay down his life for his friends."* (John 15:13)

Yes! For the joy that was set before Him, He endured the cross and despised the shame.[31] What was that joy? The joy of seeing you and me as His righteous bride; a holy bride devoid of sin. Can we ever stop thanking our Heavenly Bridegroom for cleaning us up and making us to be a beautiful bride commensurate with Him?

The Bride's Dress

Let's take an in-depth look at beautiful dress of Christ's bride. In the Gospel of Luke we read that Jesus told three consecutive stories: a lost sheep, a lost coin, and a lost son. We can all identify with these scenarios, but the third is particularly relevant to each one of us for we are the younger son.

In that story we read of a wealthy landowner who had two sons: the elder son was a good boy and the younger one a bad lad. We could say he was insolent, disrespectful, and rebellious not to mention covetous, greedy, and unprincipled. He had his eyes on his father's wealth and he wanted it NOW. He asked the father for his inheritance NOW. In effect he was saying, "I can't wait for you to die." Surprisingly, the father complied and handed over one third of the value of his estate. (In Jewish law the firstborn son receives a double portion.)

The boy wastes no time. He is off like a shot, far away from the father, far away from family to a "far country." Casting off all restraints, he has the 'so called' good time. He sleeps with prostitutes, shoots some drugs, and spends a lot of money. In fact, he spends all the money he had. Suddenly, he is destitute with no money and no food. Things go from bad to worse until we find our Jewish boy living with pigs and longing for pig food. He is literally starving. What to do? It's a dilemma. Pigs are anathema to observant Jews. Now he is so degraded that he is living with them.

We now read that *"he came to his senses."* The enormity of his conduct weighs on him. He has comprehensively blown it. He is dying. He knows the father will never accept him again as his son, but maybe, just maybe he can be a farmhand on the estate. At least he will get three meals a day and somewhere to lay his head. Emaciated and very afraid, he begins the long journey home. Over and over he rehearses his speech,

> "Father, I have sinned against heaven and before you. I am no longer worthy to be called your son. Make me like one of your hired servants." (Luke 15:18-19)

He is not hopeful. All he can expect is a good hiding and to be cut off from the family, but this boy is about to receive a rapturous reception that will change him forever.

> "When was a great way off, his father saw him and had compassion, and ran and fell on his neck and

The Bride's Dress

kissed him (again and again in the Greek). The son said, 'Father I have sinned against heaven and in your sight and am no longer worthy to be called your son.'" (vs. 20-21)

Too true, but oh, the forgiveness of the father! This is his response:

"'Bring out the BEST ROBE [The Greek word for Best Robe is stole (pronounced stol-ay')] and put it on him, put a ring on his finger and shoes on his feet. Bring out the fatted calf... let us eat and be merry; for this my son was dead and is alive again; he was lost and is found.' And they began to be merry." (vs. 22, 24)

This is your story and mine. We are that lost son. Maybe you have never been immoral. Maybe you feel fairly okay. But the Word of God tells us,

"There is none righteous, no not one. All have sinned and come short of the glory of God." And "All our righteousnesses are as filthy rags." (Romans 3:10, 23, Isaiah 64:6)

The son dragged himself back dirty, disgusting, and degraded. If you think you are not like that, then you perhaps do not understand the magnitude of our fall from grace. God resists the proud but gives grace to the humble.[32]
The father in this story is a picture of our Father in Heaven, and the four gifts he gave to the son are the gifts He gives to each one of us when we come to Him in contrition and deep repentance. Let's look at them: the best

robe (the bridal dress), a pair of shoes (slaves went barefoot; sons wore shoes), a ring (equal today to the family cheque book), and the party (a picture of the Wedding Feast of the Bridegroom and His Bride).

The Best Robe — The Bridal Dress

Jesus prefaced the three stories in Luke 15 by telling us that there is joy in heaven when one sinner repents. When you and I repent, the angels swing from the chandeliers!

This Greek word for the Best Robe (stole) is mentioned seven times in the New Testament; five times in the book of Revelation. Seven is the number of perfection. So what is this Robe? Let us take note: it is not any old robe; it is The BEST Robe. This is the robe worn by angels and martyrs. It has been described as a long white robe having a train. In the Gospel of Mark, the three women at the tomb encounter an angel, though he is there described as "a young man clothed in a long white stole."

In the sixth chapter of Revelation, we hear the cry of the martyrs as they ask the Lord to judge and avenge them.

> "Then a white robe (a stole) was given to each of them, and it was said they should rest a little longer..."

In Revelation chapter seven, the stole is mentioned three times. The beloved apostle sees *"a great multitude which no man could number, of all nations, tribes, peoples and tongues, standing before the Lamb clothed with white stole."*

The Bride's Dress

One of the Elders asks John about the multitude clothed in white, asking where they came from. John wisely answers, *"Sir you know."* The answer is given in verse fourteen:

> "These are the ones who have come out of the great tribulation and washed their robes (stole) and made them white in the blood of the Lamb."

Finally we read in Revelation 22:14, one of the closing passages of the Bible, that this is the robe that allows us access into the New Jerusalem.

> "Blessed are those who wash their robes (stole) that they may have the right to the tree of life and may enter through the gates to the city. Outside are the dogs, those who practice magic arts, the sexually immoral, the murderers, the idolaters and everyone who loves and practices falsehood." (NIV)

So we have a long white robe worn by martyrs and angels, but astonishingly also given to a 'bad boy' made clean by a forgiving father. That 'bad boy' is you. The 'bad boy' is me! The forgiving father is a type of our loving Father in Heaven. Oh, the depth of the grace of God. Our Hero Jesus took our unrighteous, our sin, and shame when He was made sin on the cross. Our beautiful robe of righteousness was freely given to us when, like 'bad boy', we came limping in repentance to our loving Father.

When we came in deep contrition acknowledging our innate wickedness and throwing ourselves on His mercy, our Father *"came running to meet us,"* arms outstretched and embraced us again and again. We surrendered our filthy garments, together with our filthy nature and instantly we were cleansed, covered, and made brand new.

> "If any man is in Christ, he is a new creation; old things are passed away, all things have become new." (2 Corinthians 5:17)

> "I will rejoice greatly in the Lord. My soul shall be joyful in my God; He has covered me with the robe of righteousness." (Isaiah 61:10)

Beautiful Bride of Christ, you are covered, mantled, and wrapped in stunning bridal garments. You have the ring on your finger and the shoes on your feet. You are spoken for, sought out, and loved so much more than you can image or think.

You are SOMEBODY, a person a great worth, a person of powerful influence. In the spirit, you are just like Jesus and one day when you see Him, you will be like Him.[33] Jesus came with GOOD NEWS. It's great news, indeed. So good we can scarcely comprehend it. Let the truth of the Word stretch your mind so that you can understand the depth, the height, and the width of God's love for you.[34]

This then is our Bridal Robe. The ring is a sign of our engagement to the Heavenly Bridegroom. Listen to these amazing words from the Apostle Paul:

> "I have betrothed you to one husband, that I may present you as a chaste virgin to Christ."
> (2 Corinthians 11:2)

> "Husbands, love your wives, just as Christ loved the church and gave Himself up for her, that He might

sanctify and cleanse her with the washing of water by the word, that He might, present her to Himself a glorious church, not having spot or wrinkle or any such thing, but that she should be HOLY and without blemish." (Ephesians 5:25–27)

The magnanimity of God's love is frankly mind-blowing. The moment we surrendered our lives totally and completely to Christ as our Lord and Saviour, that very moment we were made holy. We were made righteous. We were given our Bridal Robe as a free but costly gift.

So the robe of righteousness is a totally free, unmerited gift. But how do we keep it clean? We get the answer in the book of Revelation where twice we are told, *"These are they that have washed their robes (stole) and made them white in the blood of the Lamb."*

Oh, praise God for that most precious commodity, the untainted blood of our Saviour. This blood redeems us. It also keeps us clean.

"If we confess our sins God is faithful and just and will forgive us our sins and purify us from all unrighteousness." (1 John 1:9)

No sin will enter heaven, no unforgiveness, hatred or jealousy. So how is your Robe? Do you even have a robe? Are you indeed part of the Ekklesia , that great company of the redeemed, who together will live forever in harmony and joyful intimacy with the most glorious Heavenly Bridegroom?

14
The Wedding Feast

"On this Mount the Lord Almighty will prepare a feast of rich food for all peoples, a banquet of wine — best of meats and the finest of wine." (Isaiah 25:6 NIV)

"With fervent desire I have desired to eat this Passover with you before I suffer." (Luke 22:15)

These words break my heart. Here we have our Hero, our Lover, about to suffer the most ignominious death ever, but He is thinking of you and me. He is *"the Lamb slain from the foundation of the world"*[35] and He wants to dine with us.

"On the same night in which He was betrayed He (Jesus) took bread; and when He had given thanks, He broke it and said, 'Take, eat, this is My body which is broken for you; do this in remembrance of Me.' In the same manner He also took the cup after supper saying, 'This cup is the new covenant in My blood. This do as often as you drink it in remembrance of Me.' For as often as you eat this bread and drink this cup, you proclaim the Lord's death till He comes." (1 Corinthians 11:23- 26)

This holy meal is a foretaste of the joy-filled wedding celebration of Christ and His Bride when He will bring us into His Banqueting House and where His banner over us is love.[36] Throughout His earthly ministry our joyful Jesus loved to dine. He dined with Pharisees, publicans, tax collectors, and sinners. He dined on hillsides, in boats, and in the homes of the rich and the poor. At the wedding in Cana He turned water into wine and sorrow into joy. Jubilant Jesus set every place alight. He knew how to fast, and He knew how to feast.

Now we have the ultimate celebration:

> "A voice came from the throne saying, 'Praise God all you His servants and those who fear Him, both great and small!' And I heard, as it were, the voice of a great multitude, as the sound of many waters and as the sound of mighty thunderings, saying, 'Alleluia! For the Lord God Omnipotent reigns! Let us be glad and rejoice and give Him glory, for the marriage of the Lamb has come and the bride has made herself ready.' And to her it was granted to be arrayed in fine linen, clean and bright, for the fine linen is the righteous acts of the saints. Then he said to me, 'Write: Blessed are those who are called to the marriage supper of the Lamb.'" (Revelation 19:5-9)

Oh, don't you long to be there ? So who gets the invite? It would seem that *"many are called but few are chosen."*[37] Firstly, the bride must be ready. In his last discourses on earth Christ frequently urges us to prepare ourselves for His arrival as King of Kings and Lord of Lords.

> "Watch therefore, for you do not know what hour your Lord is coming... Therefore you also be ready, for the Son of Man is coming at an hour you do not expect." (Matthew 24:42, 44)

Secondly, only those who are properly attired will make it. In Matthew chapter twenty-two Jesus tells the parable of a king who arranged a marriage for his son. The King is God the Father, and the wedding is for His beloved Son. Amazingly, everyone is invited, but sadly, many distain to come. However, to be an accepted guest we must have the wedding garment on. For the man in the parable who was not properly dressed, there was a terrible punishment:

"Bind him hand and foot, take him away, and cast him into outer darkness; there will be weeping and gnashing of teeth. For many are called but few are chosen." (Matthew 22:13)

I pray that all of us will make it.

Let's take a look again at the bridal dress. The last chapter of Revelation tells us that only those who have washed their robes have the right to enter the Holy City. So, not only do we need the bridal robe, but it must be spotless. The Amplified Version of the Bible puts it this way:

"Blessed are those who cleanse their garments that they may have the authority and right to the tree of life and to enter in through the gates to the city." (Revelation 22:14)

As we shall see, Ephesians 5:25-32 puts it like this:

"Christ loved the church and gave Himself for her, that He might sanctify and cleanse her with the washing of water by the word, that He might present her to Himself a glorious church, not having spot or wrinkle or any such thing, but that she should be

The Wedding Feast

holy and without blemish… For we are members of His body, of His flesh and of His bones. For this reason a man shall leave his father and his mother and be joined to his wife and the two shall become one flesh. This is a great mystery, but I speak concerning Christ and the church." (Ephesians 5:25-32)

On that great day people from every nation, tribe, and tongue arrayed in bridal robes will gather together in wonder-filled praise and adoration to celebrate their Heavenly Bridegroom and to see His promise fulfilled:

"But I say to you, I will not drink of this fruit of the vine until the day when I drink it new with you in My Father's kingdom." (Matthew 26:29)

In the wonderful story of the prodigal son, the last blessing given to the reprobate was a feast. Forgiven, cleaned up, restored to sonship and properly attired, former bad boy now becomes an illustration of the bride of Christ. The last blessing he receives is a feast in his honour: *"Bring the fatted calf here and kill it, let us eat and be merry,"* a huge celebration with music, dancing, eating, drinking and great jubilation. The same parable tells us,

"There is joy in the presence of the angels of God over one sinner who repents." (Luke 15:7)

There is a phrase in this most beautiful of stories that I love: *"And they began to make merry."* The merriment, joy, and feasting in the Kingdom of God will never end as the

Ekklesia of every tribe, tongue, and nation gather as one to honour their Heavenly Bridegroom and King.

Our loving Heavenly Father has organized an extravagant party that will never end. The party is for His beloved Son. We, the once reprobate 'child' are now forgiven, cleansed and dignified, arrayed in beautiful wedding garments, anticipating an eternity of unmitigated joy in the Presence of our Holy Father, the mystical union with His Only Son in the company of uncountable myriads of holy angels.

Throughout His earthly ministry the Son of God loved to feast. He dined with rich and poor, publicans, Pharisees and close friends. He fed multitudes on hillsides and turned water into wine at the wedding in Cana. Not only was He a man of sorrows, but also a man of celebration. He could dance and leap for joy. Now the joyful Father of Jubilant Jesus invites you and me to the greatest party of all time: a party that will last throughout eternity.

Will you be there?

"God so loved the world that He gave His only begotten Son that whosoever believes in Him should not perish but have everlasting life." (John 3:16)

15
Our Eternal Home

In the Jewish culture, parents would seek for a bride for their son or they would employ a matchmaker, a Shadkah. The bride was to be morally, physically, and spiritually compatible to the groom. Today we see the Holy Spirit as our Matchmaker gently wooing us to Christ.

Next, a Ketubah or covenant, was drawn up. This would be negotiated and agreed by both parties. It would guarantee the bride certain rights and privileges. It was a document often beautifully written by a calligrapher to be framed and displayed in the nuptial home. This still happens today. It was a binding legal agreement as in a modern wedding when both bride and groom take a solemn vow, sealed with an oath to give ourselves to each and all our worldly goods; to love and cherish one another "until death do us part." This Ketubah would cement the engagement, the betrothal. But the actual marriage would not take place until one year later. However the covenant could not be broken except by divorce, which is why when Joseph, the husband of Mary, discovered that she was pregnant he was minded "to put her away quietly" as he believed she had violated the covenant made between them.

Our 'ketubah' is the whole of Scripture. *"In the volume of the book it is written of Me,"* declares our Bridegroom. If the Old Testament is the husbandly love of God for His people Israel, then the New Testament is the covenantal passion of Christ for His Bride, the church. This is where we, the Bride, find ourselves to be, as the Apostle Paul tells us:

"I have betrothed you to one husband, that I may present you as a chaste virgin to Christ." (2 Corinthians 11:2)

During the period of separation and preparation both bride and groom would be eagerly awaiting the day of consummation. The groom would be busy preparing a dwelling place for his bride. The usual place would be in the house or compound of his father. Right now the Lord Jesus is doing just that:

"Let not your heart be troubled. In My Father's house are many mansions (or dwellings) ... I go to prepare a place for you. And if I go and prepare a place for you, I will come again and receive you to Myself; that where I am, there you may be also." (John 14:1-3)

What a day that will be! What a place that will be! He is coming back for His beautiful bride! He has prepared a place for us. He is eagerly waiting for the fulfillment of all His desires. Are we excited? Are we prepared? Are our "lamps" burning with the oil of the Holy Spirit? Think of our destiny:

"Eye has not seen, nor ear heard, nor have entered into the heart of man the things which God has prepared for those who love Him." (1 Corinthians 2:9)

Isaiah puts it like this:

"Behold I create a new heavens and a new earth... Be glad and rejoice forever in what I create; for behold I create Jerusalem as a rejoicing and her people a joy. I will rejoice in Jerusalem and joy in My people; the voice of weeping shall no longer be heard in her, nor the voice of crying." (Isaiah 65:17-19)

The Bible is relatively silent about our final dwelling place. King David saw that it would be a place of goodness and mercy and that he would dwell in the house of the Lord forever. Saint Paul tells us that he was snatched up into the third heaven and into Paradise where he heard *"...inexpressible words which it is not lawful for man to utter."*[38] Revelation 21 states:

"I saw a new heaven and a new earth for the first heaven had passed away. I, John, saw the holy city, New Jerusalem, coming down out of heaven prepared as a bride adorned for her husband. And I heard a loud voice saying, 'Behold the tabernacle of God is with men, and He will dwell with them, and they shall be His people. God Himself will be with them and be their God. And God will wipe away every tear from their eyes; there shall be no more death, nor sorrow, nor crying. There shall be no more pain for the former things have passed away.' Then He who sat on the throne said, 'Behold I make all things new.'"

There is plenty of mystery there, but imagine a place of perfection, no sin, no sadness, no Satan. We have eternity to discover the wonders of our final home. However, it is not the environment that will so much excite us but our Father, our Creator, the Holy Spirit, our Matchmaker and our Lord Jesus Christ revealed in all His brilliance — the One who lights up the entire universe with the splendour of His glory. No longer the calloused carpenter, but the King of Kings and Lord of Lords. Every eye will see Him, every knee will bow before Him, and every tongue will confess that Jesus Christ is Lord to the glory of God.

The end of all things is at hand. The Lord Jesus is coming soon. God's Secret Agent has conquered! With one spectacular act of self-giving, He has disposed of death, decay, and sin forever. He is coming again to make all things new! There will be a New Heavens and a New Earth. The Second Adam will initiate a new Eden more glorious than the first.

He is coming for a bride dazzling in holiness, spotless and blameless. He is coming for those who have endured trials yet have not compromised. He is coming with a massive entourage of mighty angels. He is coming…

> "…in flaming fire taking vengeance on those who do not know God, and on those who do not obey the gospel of our Lord Jesus Christ. These shall be punished with everlasting destruction from the presence of the Lord and from the glory of His power." (2 Thessalonians 1:7-10)

For those of us who know and love and serve him, He

> "…will descend with a shout, with the voice of an archangel and with the trumpet of God. And the dead in Christ shall rise first. Then we who are alive and remain shall be caught up together with them in the clouds to meet the Lord in the air. So shall we always be with the Lord. Therefore comfort one another with these words." (1 Thessalonians 4:16-18)

We are told to watch for we do not know what hour our Lord is coming. Jesus Himself tells us, *"Surely I am coming quickly."* (Revelation 22:20) May we respond with love and longing:

"Amen. Even so, come, Lord Jesus!"

Epilogue

How Do We, the Bride, Prepare to Meet our Eternal Bridegroom?

Will you be ready on that great day when the Lord will return with a shout of triumph to claim His bride—the one for whom He laid down His life, becoming the ultimate sacrifice?

Will you say with Rebekah, *"I will go. I will leave everything to love and serve this King?"*

Will you, like Ruth declare, *"Your people shall be my people, Your God shall be my God. Where You go, I will go. I give You my lifelong devotion?"* And will you say, *"You are my nearest Kinsman. Spread the corner of Your garment over me."*?

Or with David, *"One thing have I desired, that will I seek after, that I may dwell in the house of the Lord all the days of my life to behold the beauty of the Lord and to inquire in His tabernacle?"*

With you, like Bathsheba, extend blanket forgiveness to a man who raped you, killed your husband, and caused your baby to die? Can we who have been forgiven much overcome evil with the love that covers a multitude of sins?

Or can we be daring and valiant like Esther? Can we say, *"If I perish, I perish."*

Or with Paul, *"I am crucified with Christ, nevertheless I live, but the life I now live, I live by faith in the Son of God who loved me and gave Himself for me."*

Can we come like the Prodigal Son, humbly to our Heavenly Father confessing, *"Father I have sinned against heaven and in Your sight. I am no longer worthy to be Your son?"* Do we understand that the rapturous welcome from the Father continues for us daily and that the party goes on throughout all eternity?

Have you ever thought that the Lord Jesus left His comfort zone with His Father to rescue YOU? He is not willing that any should perish, but that all (of us) should come to repentance. Repentance is the gateway to eternal life with Christ. Each one of us has sinned and come short of the glory of God. Jesus cannot be joined to a sinful bride. He loves you and me so much that He gave His very life and shed His blood to clean us up and make us his holy bride.

"Without the shedding of blood there is no remission of sin." (Hebrews 9:22)

Step One: Come to Him today. Acknowledge your sin-filled nature. Humbly ask Him for forgiveness and instantly you will be clean.

Step Two: Like Ruth and Rebekah, tell Him you are willing to hand over the lordship of your life to Him. What He wants you to do, you will do. Where He directs, you will go. Surrender your life to Him. You will experience the joy of sins forgiven and a brand-new life that will never end.

Epilogue

You will have a brand-new Bridegroom, a new relationship with God as your Father, and the Holy Spirit as your constant Guide and Companion.

Step Three: Love this wonderful Heavenly Bridegroom with all your heart. Read His love letter to you and say with the Shulamite:

> "Set me as a seal upon Your heart, as a seal upon Your arm for love is as strong as death." (Song of Solomon 8:6)

God bless you. See you on that Great Day!

> "Now unto Him who is able to keep you from falling, and to present you faultless before the presence of His glory with exceeding joy, to the only wise God our Saviour be glory and majesty, dominion and power, both now and forever. Amen." (Jude 1:24-25)

Catherine

If you have taken these steps, I would love to rejoice with you. Email me at Catherine.jinadu@btinternet.com

Endnotes

[1] Winston Churchill quote on a drawing. Library of Congress Prints and Photographs Division Washington, D.C. 20540 USA
http://hdl.loc.gov/loc.pnp/pp.print

[2] Hebrews 10:7

[3] Ephesians 3:14

[4] Hebrews 1:3

[5] Ephesians 1:4

[6] Genesis 1:28

[7] Isaiah 14:12-18 Before he rebelled against the Most High Satan or Lucifer was the anointed cherub that covers. He can appear as an angel of light.

[8] Romans 3:10

[9] The Book of Common Prayer was published by Archbishop Thomas Cranmer in 1549. It is totally based on Scripture and is still used in the updated version by the Anglican Church and many other churches today. Archbishop Cranmer was tried for heresy by Queen Mary who was a staunch Catholic. He was burnt at the state in 1556. His final words were, *"Lord Jesus receive my spirit... I see the heavens opened and Jesus Christ standing at the right hand of God."* Certainly, he did not turn back.

[10] The lineage of Boaz: His father was Salmon and his mother Rahab, the former Canaanite prostitute. His grandfather was Nashon, son of Amminadab, leader of the tribe of Judah. (Matthew 1:4, 5)

[11] Deuteronomy 25:5-9. The Levirate Law

[12] Ruth 3:9

[13] Psalm 147:4

[14] In 2 Samuel 11 we have a full account of David's sins and his absence from the battlefield of Rabbah. After his repentance, the second account of the battle is found in 1 Chronicles 20. There are only 3 verses and no mention of the crimes. They have been blotted out from his record. David assures us of this in Ps 103: 11,12, *"For as the heavens are high above the earth, so great is His mercy towards those who fear Him, As far as the east is from the west so far has He removed our transgressions from us."*

[15] 1 The Mikvah. According to the law given to Moses in Leviticus 15:19 Jewish women were considered unclean after menstruation. They were to take a ritual bath immersing themselves three times in rainwater and not resume intimate relations with their husbands for a further seven days. We assume there was a tub of rainwater on the flat roof of her house. She did this innocently. She did not know that she was being watched.

[16] 2 Samuel 23:34. Eliam is listed as one of David's mighty men. His father is Ahitophel, David's Counsellor.

THE ULTIMATE WEDDING

[17] David's first wife was Michal, daughter of King Saul, followed by Ahinoam, Abigail, Macaah, Haggith, Abital, Eglah and nine other unnamed wives all who bore sons. 2 Chronicles 3:1-9

[18] *"You are the man!"* (2 Samuel 12:7) Only David is accused of adultery and murder by Almighty God through the prophet Nathan. Bathsheba is never condemned.

[19] Four dead sons: Daniel (Chileb) son of Abigail dies in infancy as does the unnamed son born to Bathsheba. Ammon, the firstborn son is murdered by his half-brother Absalom. Rebellious Absalom is killed by Joab. The eldest surviving son is Adonijah who would have been over forty years old at the time of David's death.

[20] Solomon is the author of Proverbs, Ecclesiastes, Song of Songs and two Psalms. 'Tanakh' is the Hebrew word for the Old Testament.

[21] Matthew 1 shows that the genealogy of Joseph, the husband of Mary, comes through Solomon. In Luke 3, the genealogy of Jesus comes through Nathan (v. 32). Bathsheba, what a legacy!

[22] 1 Kings 2:19, 1 Kings 11:6

[23] Ahasuerus, or Xerxes succeeded Darius 1 in 485 BC as king of Persia. His Empire extended from India to Ethiopia, encompassing 127 nations. He was a weak king, a drunkard, and a womanizer. But through the costly intervention of the entire Jewish population, all that was to change.

[24] What we read in the book of Hebrews could well be said of Esther: *"...who through faith subdued kingdoms, worked righteousness, obtained promises, stopped the mouth of lions, quenched the violence of fire, escaped the edge of the sword."* (Hebrews 11:33, 34)

[25] *"If I have found favor in the sight of the king, and if it pleases the king to grant my petition and fulfill my request, then let the king and Haman come to the banquet which I will prepare for them, and tomorrow I will do as the king has said."* (Esther 5:8)

[26] *"Behold! The Lamb of God who takes away the sin of the world!"* (John 1:29)

[27] Isaiah 64:6

[28] Colossians 2:11-15

[29] Revelation 1:18

[30] *O Little Town of Bethlehem* - United Methodist Hymnal #230

[31] Hebrews 12:2

[32] 1 Peter 5:5

[33] 1 John 3:2

[34] Ephesians 3:18

[35] Revelation 13:8

[36] Song of Solomon 2:4

[37] Matthew 22:14

[38] 2 Corinthians 12:2-4

About the Author

Catherine Anne (Kate) Jinadu is the founder and co-director of the charity Liberty — Making People Free, and President of Covenant Women International. Kate is the wife of Paul, the General Overseer of the New Covenant Church, which operates in many countries. She is the author of *Foundations for Christian Marriage, Tamar, Bathsheba,* and *Dancing on the Waves With Jesus.*

www.nccworld.org

Catherine.jinadu@btinternet.com

Printed in Great Britain
by Amazon